You with Your Young Reader

You with Your Young Reader

One-Year Bible Reader for Parent and Child

Leon D. Engman

WIPF & STOCK · Eugene, Oregon

YOU WITH YOUR YOUNG READER
One-Year Bible Reader for Parent and Child

Copyright © 2022 Leon D. Engman. All rights reserved. Except for brief quotations in critical publications or reviews, no part of this book may be reproduced in any manner without prior written permission from the publisher. Write: Permissions, Wipf and Stock Publishers, 199 W. 8th Ave., Suite 3, Eugene, OR 97401.

Wipf & Stock
An Imprint of Wipf and Stock Publishers
199 W. 8th Ave., Suite 3
Eugene, OR 97401

www.wipfandstock.com

PAPERBACK ISBN: 978-1-6667-1192-9
HARDCOVER ISBN: 978-1-6667-1193-6
EBOOK ISBN: 978-1-6667-1194-3

03/28/22

For my favorite young readers:
Magdalena, Iona, Anastasia, Helena, and Signe.

> Stand at the crossroads and look. Ask about the pathway of ancient days, "where is the good way?" then walk in it, and you will find a resting place for your souls.
>
> —JEREMIAH 6:16

> Persistently teach these words to your children. Speak of them when you sit in your house, when you walk along the way, when you lie down, and when you rise up.
>
> —DEUTERONOMY 6:7

Contents

Preface | ix
Introduction | xi

Week 1
    Reading 1 | 2
    Reading 2 | 4
    Reading 3 | 6

Week 2
    Reading 1 | 8
    Reading 2 | 10
    Reading 3 | 12

Week 3
    Reading 1 | 14
    Reading 2 | 16
    Reading 3 | 18

Week 4
    Reading 1 | 20
    Reading 2 | 22
    Reading 3 | 24

Week 5
    Reading 1 | 26
    Reading 2 | 28
    Reading 3 | 30

Week 6
    Reading 1 | 32
    Reading 2 | 34
    Reading 3 | 36

Week 7
    Reading 1 | 38
    Reading 2 | 40
    Reading 3 | 42

Week 8
    Reading 1 | 44
    Reading 2 | 46
    Reading 3 | 48

Week 9
    Reading 1 | 50
    Reading 2 | 52
    Reading 3 | 54

Week 10
    Reading 1 | 56
    Reading 2 | 58
    Reading 3 | 60

Week 11
    Reading 1 | 62
    Reading 2 | 64
    Reading 3 | 66

Week 12
    Reading 1 | 68
    Reading 2 | 70
    Reading 3 | 72

Week 13
    Reading 1 | 74
    Reading 2 | 76
    Reading 3 | 78

Week 14
    Reading 1 | 80
    Reading 2 | 82
    Reading 3 | 84

Week 15
    Reading 1 | 86
    Reading 2 | 88
    Reading 3 | 90

Week 16
- Reading 1 | 92
- Reading 2 | 94
- Reading 3 | 96

Week 17
- Reading 1 | 98
- Reading 2 | 100
- Reading 3 | 102

Week 18
- Reading 1 | 104
- Reading 2 | 106
- Reading 3 | 108

Week 19
- Reading 1 | 110
- Reading 2 | 112
- Reading 3 | 114

Week 20
- Reading 1 | 116
- Reading 2 | 118
- Reading 3 | 120

Week 21
- Reading 1 | 122
- Reading 2 | 124
- Reading 3 | 126

Week 22
- Reading 1 | 128
- Reading 2 | 130
- Reading 3 | 132

Week 23
- Reading 1 | 134
- Reading 2 | 136
- Reading 3 | 138

Week 24
- Reading 1 | 140
- Reading 2 | 142
- Reading 3 | 144

Week 25
- Reading 1 | 146
- Reading 2 | 148
- Reading 3 | 150

Week 26
- Reading 1 | 152
- Reading 2 | 154
- Reading 3 | 156

Week 27
- Reading 1 | 158
- Reading 2 | 160
- Reading 3 | 162

Week 28
- Reading 1 | 164
- Reading 2 | 166
- Reading 3 | 168

Week 29
- Reading 1 | 170
- Reading 2 | 172
- Reading 3 | 174

Week 30
- Reading 1 | 176
- Reading 2 | 178
- Reading 3 | 180

Week 31
- Reading 1 | 182
- Reading 2 | 184
- Reading 3 | 186

Week 32
- Reading 1 | 188
- Reading 2 | 190
- Reading 3 | 192

Week 33
- Reading 1 | 194
- Reading 2 | 196
- Reading 3 | 198

Week 34
- Reading 1 | 200
- Reading 2 | 202
- Reading 3 | 204

Week 35
- Reading 1 | 206
- Reading 2 | 208
- Reading 3 | 210

Week 36
- Reading 1 | 212
- Reading 2 | 214
- Reading 3 | 216

Week 37
- Reading 1 | 218
- Reading 2 | 220
- Reading 3 | 222

Week 38
- Reading 1 | 224
- Reading 2 | 226
- Reading 3 | 228

Week 39
- Reading 1 | 230
- Reading 2 | 232
- Reading 3 | 234

Week 40
    Reading 1 | 236
    Reading 2 | 238
    Reading 3 | 240

Week 41
    Reading 1 | 242
    Reading 2 | 244
    Reading 3 | 246

Week 42
    Reading 1 | 248
    Reading 2 | 250
    Reading 3 | 252

Week 43
    Reading 1 | 254
    Reading 2 | 256
    Reading 3 | 258

Week 44
    Reading 1 | 260
    Reading 2 | 262
    Reading 3 | 264

Week 45
    Reading 1 | 266
    Reading 2 | 268
    Reading 3 | 270

Week 46
    Reading 1 | 272
    Reading 2 | 274
    Reading 3 | 276

Week 47
    Reading 1 | 278
    Reading 2 | 280
    Reading 3 | 282

Week 48
    Reading 1 | 284
    Reading 2 | 286
    Reading 3 | 288

Week 49
    Reading 1 | 290
    Reading 2 | 292
    Reading 3 | 294

Week 50
    Reading 1 | 296
    Reading 2 | 298
    Reading 3 | 300

Week 51
    Reading 1 | 302
    Reading 2 | 304
    Reading 3 | 306

Week 52
    Reading 1 | 308
    Reading 2 | 310
    Reading 3 | 312

Preface

This parent-and-child Bible reader has deeper roots than first glance may reveal. Much of New Testament biblical theology is based on reading the Bible as a story. Paul and the writer of Hebrews stress the priority of the promise to Abraham over the Law of Moses. The priority is chronology-driven: Abraham and Melchizedek come before Moses and Levi in the story. Moses and the law are an important, eternal, but parenthetical part of the bigger story of the promised Messiah, Jesus.

For centuries the synagogue and church drowned each other out by pounding the drum of their own worship lectionaries. The synagogue lectionaries are built around the five books of Moses. The church lectionaries are built around the four Gospels. They were designed, in part, as bulwarks against one another. The whole of the Bible story is largely understated or missing in both.

You with Your Young Reader is built on a lectionary that goes through the Bible story interwoven with the Bible's ongoing internal (intertextual) conversation about what has already happened and what is promised ahead. This lectionary was written, used in worship service for nine years (three three-year cycles) in an evangelical free church, continuously modified, and then analyzed by academic Bible specialists as part of the author's doctoral project at Trinity Evangelical Divinity School.

This application of the Bible story lectionary grows out of a current pressing need. The institutions we have long relied on to teach our children seem less trustworthy to us of late. There is a positive side: Scripture tells us parents that we are primarily responsible for teaching our children no matter what else is going on. We have been properly reminded of that in the

PREFACE

recent years of social and political turmoil. We parents have an obligation to educate our children.

This is not a children's book as such. It is for parents introducing their newly literate child to the world of reading and thinking with Scripture. It also works well as an individual or group devotional for all ages. But it is specifically designed as something a dad or mom can do with a child that will bond their lives together. They will have a reason and a way to spend time interacting with one another on what life with God means.

Many thanks to the parents and children who tested this reader and gave insightful feedback. We are entering a new era that is calling us to reestablish some foundational ancient practices into our flitting high-tech existence. This reader provides a pathway for our children to walk on with strength and confidence into the strange world they are inheriting.

Introduction

The Bible is the foundational document of western culture. To read it is to be being educated. To *ignore* it is to be *ignorant*. Literacy advanced rapidly in the western world when people began to have access to the Bible in their mother tongue. Ironically, Bible knowledge has been intentionally buried and abandoned lately in most sectors of public life in the US; a decision to be ignorant.

Many parents have a sense that there is something useful and good in the Bible for our children but have no idea what to do about it. The Bible is a large book from the ancient world. We know it is important, but to approach it is intimidating. It is like showing a hungry person a cow or a field of wheat: *I see that this could be nourishment, but how do I feed myself and my family with this*? It takes guidance and work.

Teaching our children is basic to being human, and one of the great responsibilities of serving the Lord. The Scriptures are full of reminders that the duty of each generation is to pass God's word on to the next (Deuteronomy 6:7, 20-25). Regardless of school or church choices, the duty of parents remains. Most parents feel that burden keenly. We are ultimately responsible for our children. This book is intended to be a tool in the hand of those willing to engage the challenging but doable task of bringing God's rich nutrition into our children's lives as well as our own.

The Design

This not a children's book *per se*. It is a parent's book to help children beginning to read the Bible for the first time. It has three Bible reading sessions for each week with leader notes and discussion questions. It introduces the parent and child to the major storyline, characters, and inner conversations of the Bible in one year. It is designed with parent-child interaction in mind, but it can be used in a variety of situations and levels of reading ability. It can be engaged as an individual or in groups for personal spiritual growth and discipleship.

The reader is set up for three readings each week, knowing that getting together every single day can become impossible and the project quickly abandoned. Three readings a week has been recognized as a good pace for together Bible reading since ancient times. Life is only predictable to a certain level. This flexibility allows for life's flow. At three times per week, we are more likely to see the project through, especially if it involves getting two or more people together, even in the same house.

Each reading has a Bible story that is introduced by a one-to-two sentence connecting statement. That statement is connected to the previous reading's story and to the larger Bible story. Then each story is followed by a second, shorter passage—from the non-story parts of the Bible—that describes, interprets, sings, applies the story directly, or applies principles from the story. This second, shorter passage shows the interconnected fabric, the inside conversation, of the Bible. It shows how deeply interwoven God's word is. This shorter passage is also introduced by a connecting statement that ties it to the story. This passage is also followed by discussion-starter questions. The whole time taken is usually around fifteen minutes.

How to Use the Reader

The first thing is to find a Bible translation in modern English that your child can read and likes. Children's ability to understand a text being read is often higher than their actual read-out-loud skills. So, depending on your situation, either one of you could read the Bible text out loud or trade back and forth on any given day. Children may be reluctant to read at first but will soon grow to love having an audience to read to. Remember, it is about child-parent interaction. Keep it positive and enjoyable, with lots of praise.

Reading the Bible text helps improve your child's reading skills. The questions are intentionally a little challenging, but still engaging, for grade-school readers. That allows you, as parent, to bring your child's thinking up into new places.

INTRODUCTION

For the parent a useful approach to each reading might be to—as your child is looking up the first passage in the Bible—scan the Bible passages, review the leader notes, and then go back to the top of the page for that day. Then, with your child, work down the page. Read the Bible Story connection statement (in **bold type**), the passage, and discuss the questions. Then do the same for the Bible Conversation connection statement, passage, and questions. The Leader Notes will prepare the parent for guiding the reading and the questions.

The questions are designed to guide the conversation within the intention of the passage. Your child will likely ask questions that are not part of the message of the text. Those questions are important because that is where your child's understanding is. They are part of the conversation but discussed in relation to its intended meaning. All matters will not be settled at the time of the reading but will spark ongoing conversation.

Part of the education going on is that not every important Bible or life question has a clear, clean answer. The ability to live with uncertainty or open-ended questions but still have strong faith in what is clear is a large part of growing up.

This journey with your child is an ancient, central part of biblical parenting. Dads and moms can take this on as an important, doable, quantifiable project with their kids. It is low-hanging fruit, an easy win. It will be remembered and is a life-changer for all involved.

This reader works on different levels, like the Bible does. Most of the questions can be answered—perhaps differently—in a grade-schooler's world and an adult's. You can take your child's question as deep as you need. The questions are not about getting right answers as much as finding doorways into conversations about where you and your child are in life.

If we regard Bible reading and conversation as lifelong companions, we may engage entirely new sets of questions each time we come to the same passage at different points of our life. There is no need to be stuck or frustrated—we learn and teach by overcoming each obstacle as we approach it. We ask many questions and sometimes leave questions unanswered. Jesus did that plenty.

This reader is not just a one-and-done guide. There is no expiration date! It can be used over and over along the way, strengthening understanding, competency, and faith. God will use your family to change the world. It starts here in his Word. Bon voyage!

WEEK 1

Reading 1

BIBLE STORY

The creation account is the beginning of the Bible, the Law of Moses, and the history of humans.

Genesis 1:1—2:3

How are people and animals the same and different?

Why do we think about our beginnings? Do animals? Why?

Who already exists at the beginning and who does not? What difference does that make?

What parts of this creation account describe the way we still live today?

BIBLE CONVERSATION

A long time later, God reveals more about the creation and before.

John 1:1–5, 10-14

Who is the Word?

How many titles and names for Jesus are in John 1? (Take a quick look and count.)

How do we become a child of God (John 1:12)?

WEEK 1: READING 1

Leader Notes

The seven-day creation account is a patterned, literary tapestry. It is more of an art piece than a science text, on purpose. It accounts for the totality of human existence, space, time, and life inside the thin blue band (what the atmosphere looks like from space) around the planet we call Earth. It begins human history and sets a frame for all our interactions with God, nature, and other living beings. The main point is that everything we know, understand, and are is from God. The creation is an act of his love that brings life and order from chaos. This account is not about how God created but why he created good things. Everything he created—animals, stars, moon, sun—has been worshipped by people. This account is about how all these things are less than the creator and not worthy of our worship. We are higher in value than the idols we worship because we are made in the Creator's image.

Questions about cavemen and dinosaurs are good questions. The Bible does not address those directly, but it does not push them out of possibility either. It intentionally leaves some doors ajar. We explore those topics in other realms, but the Bible focuses on things it considers central to its message.

John the apostle (not the baptizer) starts his Gospel with "In the beginning." It is a clear reference to Genesis 1. He wants us to know that this Jesus is not just an afterthought. He is behind everything since before the beginning. He is now revealed as the center of God's plan for bringing all people back into relationship with himself.

WEEK 1

Reading 2

BIBLE STORY

After laying out the greatness of creation, the writer begins the story of man and woman and their first temple of worship, the garden.

Genesis 2:4–25

What was incredibly great about life in the garden (Genesis 2:16)?

How do we know that God wants good things for us?

Why does God make only one law that the man and the woman can break if they choose (Genesis 2:17)?

BIBLE CONVERSATION

God later reveals another amazing foundation stone of his creation.

Proverbs 8:12–14, 22–31; 9:1–6

Wisdom is described as a woman we should listen to. Do you know anyone like that?

Why does God delight in wisdom?

Why is wisdom—knowing about good and bad—such an important part of creation?

WEEK 1: READING 2

Leader Notes

The garden was a place of protection. It was heaven on earth, a place to be with God. In keeping with our nature, "you will surely die" catches our attention. It overshadows the generous, open invitation to eat freely from every tree except this one. We cannot help but focus on the one tree we are not allowed to have. If God gave them no choice, they would not love God of their own freewill, they would only do what they knew to do, like the animals. So, he gives them a choice.

Creation is chock full of wisdom, but the man and woman are apparently not yet ready for that kind of wisdom. Wisdom is a big topic in the Bible. It ranges from being skillful at our craft, clever in our dealings, all the way to being like God. The role of being a parent is a godlike role.

WEEK 1

Reading 3

BIBLE STORY

In the first generation of man and woman our troubles begin.

Genesis 3

If wisdom is behind all creation, why is it wrong for the woman to seek wisdom for herself (Genesis 3:6)?

How does the man and woman's decision made in the garden affect us to this day?

What is the glimmer of hope in this sad story (Genesis 3:15)?

BIBLE CONVERSATION

The ongoing war between the seed of the woman and the snake rages on to us and beyond. It encompasses all of humanity and the heavens.

Revelation 12

What woman and child are the most important ones in the Bible?

The snake is already defeated. Why does he work so hard at harming us?

Who do we find out the snake is?

WEEK 1: READING 3

Leader Notes

The woman is attracted and tempted by the offer of wisdom that will make her like God. Children imitate their parents, but are still children. Adam and Eve's innocence is like that of children or animals, unashamed of their nakedness. Genesis 3:15 speaks of an ongoing conflict between humans and the snake. The humans will win, but at a great cost.

The snake is revealed, eventually, to be the dragon, the devil. The seed of the woman that wins the conflict for all people is revealed to be Jesus the Messiah. The Revelation passage is apocalyptic literature, full of symbols. The point is that everything was at stake way back in the garden. The enemy is real, and the victory is only won by God himself coming into his own creation as one of us.

WEEK 2

Reading 1

BIBLE STORY

After being exiled from the garden, the man and the woman watch their children make choices for themselves. The man and woman now experience some of the sadness God apparently felt watching them choose.

Genesis 4

How do Cain's people turn out, living away from the Lord (Genesis 4:24)?

In which person and in whose technology do Cain's people trust? (Clue: look in the mirror.)

What characterizes Seth's people (Genesis 4:26)? Why is that important?

BIBLE CONVERSATION

Near the end of the Bible, John helps us understand Adam and Eve's children and the choices they made.

1 John 3:10–13

What do our choices reflect about our hearts?

How do we choose which humanity—Cain or Seth—to belong to?

WEEK 2: READING 1

Leader Notes

Two humanities emerge in Genesis 4: those relying on themselves and those calling on the name of the Lord. Both humanities come from the same parents. It is not genetics. It is their choices.

The Bible is not for or against technology, but technology emerges as a magnifier of human efforts, good and bad. It becomes a way for humans to survive together away from God. The Bible is already raising questions it does not answer. It wants us to keep reading, listening, thinking, and acting. Some questions raised are answered later, some are never answered. The Bible wants us to join a lifelong conversation with our creator, like children with parents.

The New Testament is a reading of the Old Testament in the light of having seen Jesus the Messiah. John's letter goes back to Genesis 4 to address the two humanities. The people of Seth, who took the place of Abel, now call on the name of the Lord through the ultimate seed of the woman, Jesus the Messiah.

WEEK 2

Reading 2

BIBLE STORY

With the birth of Seth, God begins a long line of people who call on him. That line goes from Adam to the time of Noah, when God is having a problem with the rest of humanity.

Genesis 5:1–5; 5:28—6:22

What are corruption and violence? Why are they so bad?

Why is God sad about our behavior (Genesis 6:5–6, 11–12)?

Have any of us disappointed our parents by our bad behavior?

BIBLE CONVERSATION

Paul, much later, explains about the vast numbers of people who choose to reject God.

Romans 1:16–23

Why is God and his goodness obvious to everyone?

Why do so many people choose to ignore their creator?

Why does God give us choices instead of programming us like robots?

WEEK 2: READING 2

Leader Notes

Readers often focus on the sons of God and the Nephilim (fallen ones) in Genesis 6:2–4 and later in the Torah. The Bible mentions them but does not explain. Many books are written speculating on what the Bible never makes clear. The part we often miss is the main, obvious thing that follows: the Lord is sorry he made us because of our behavior and evil hearts. That is a big deal and we should be focused on it.

Human corruption and violence are the reasons why God destroyed everything and everyone in the flood. Those remain the central characteristics of human interaction to this day. God remains sad about it to this day, but he rejoices in the redeemed hearts of his children, those who follow Jesus.

Paul, in Romans, says that the creation all around us makes the existence and goodness of God obvious to all. The gospel of Jesus is now the dividing line between the humanities, not race, creed, or gender. Creation reveals God to all people. Jesus, the living Word of God, reveals exactly who God is and what he wants. There are still two humanities; those who call on the name of the Lord and those who do not. Both are still the only real choices.

WEEK 2

Reading 3

BIBLE STORY

God shuts Noah, from the line of Seth, and his family into a safe place, away from the coming judgment of water.

Genesis 7

When is it *good* to pay close attention (Genesis 7:5, 16)?

When is it *wise* to be different than everyone else?

When is it *critical* to be in the safe place God provides?

BIBLE CONVERSATION

We find out later that one of God's judgments is being left to do whatever we want.

Romans 1:24–32

What does it mean when our parents tell us the right thing to do?

What does it mean that "God gave them over" (Romans 1:24, 26, 28)?

Why is it not good when no one tells us the bad things we do are wrong?

WEEK 2: READING 3

Leader Notes

The ark is a place for God's people to safely hide while he brings judgment on the disobedient world. There will be many safe places in the Bible story. The garden was a safe place from the world around. The town of Zoar will be safe from the judgment of Sodom and Gomorrah. The houses with the blood of the Passover lamb will be safe places from the slaying of the firstborn in Egypt. Ultimately, Jesus will be our safe place from the coming judgment on the whole world.

When God is very specific, we need to pay particular attention. He gave very specific instructions about the ark. He gives very specific instructions now about our allegiance to Jesus the King. If we choose something vague like, "just have faith in something," we are not paying attention.

In Romans, Paul reminds us that God is very specific about the design of man and woman. When we repurpose that design to suit our own desires, and feelings, we are not paying attention. When we break the foundations laid for our existence, it is a sign that we are not paying attention to our creator.

Having someone who cares enough to tell us when we are off course is of great value if we trust that someone. If no one tells us anything because we never listen, we are in trouble. If we listen to voices we should not trust, like the snake in the garden, we are in trouble.

In judgment, what is at stake is like the difference between our parent speaking uncomfortable truth in the living room, and a judge pronouncing a prison sentence on us in a court: big difference! Keep the conversation with our parents and stay out of the courtroom! We can have God as loving father or judge; it is our choice!

WEEK 3

Reading 1

BIBLE STORY

After the floodwaters come on the earth, Noah and his family are in the safe ark with the animals for a long time.

Genesis 8

What might it mean that "God remembered Noah?" Did he ever forget?

When we feel forgotten at times, are we?

What sad thing does God know about us (Genesis 8:21)?

BIBLE CONVERSATION

God always provides a safe place for his people when he judges the world, even now.

Romans 2:1–8

If we think we are better than someone else, what are we doing to ourselves (Romans 2:1)?

Why is doing the right thing different than just being better than someone else (Romans 2:7)?

WEEK 3: READING 1

Leader Notes

God has the right to judge his creation. He did, and he will do it again. Noah is a second creation story with the same commands to be fruitful and multiply. The Lord decides to let things continue as they are—without another flood—because this thing in our hearts will not get better by itself, or by trying harder.

Noah is in the line of Seth. The flood sweeps Cain's people away. With only righteous Noah's family to start over, will things be alright now? (Spoiler alert: no, because it is not genetics. It is in every human heart, even Noah's.)

Paul says we cannot be safe from judgment by being better than someone else. We have to keep our eyes on the Lord, listening and following. Doing that, we will meet Jesus and he will take us where we are safe and much more.

WEEK 3

Reading 2

BIBLE STORY

After the flood, with a new creation, Noah fails like Adam and there is another curse. Humanity quickly ends up in the same situation as before.

Genesis 9; 11:1–9

In the logic of the flood story, what happens to the garden and the tree of life?

What is true about people then and now (Genesis 11:4)?

Why does God again seem rather sad, like when he sent Adam and Eve out of the garden (Genesis 3:21–23; 11:5–6)?

BIBLE CONVERSATION

It turns out that we all have the same problem as Adam, and God has a solution that works for all of us, but we must choose it.

Romans 3:21–26

If we can have a good and right relationship with God, why should we want that?

What does it mean to have faith and to believe in Jesus the Messiah? Is it more than just acknowledging his existence?

If Messiah means "anointed one," which is the King, what is the proper response to our King?

WEEK 3: READING 2

Leader Notes

Genesis 9 is creation 2.0. The garden and the tree of life are apparently swept away in the flood. This new creation begins with the same blessings and has a new law about not consuming animal blood and not spilling human blood. God makes a promise to never again bring a flood. In another scene involving fruit (Noah's wine), the fall happens again, and another curse is given. Then the genealogy that started in chapter 5 is ended at the end of Noah's life.

Chapter 11 is about another people of Cain arising, this time from Noah's bloodlines. It is in all of us. The tower of Babel is a symbol of man's high-tech dreams of all humanity speaking as one voice. God is not impressed.

Paul says that we still have the same problem as we did before the flood and at the tower; our advanced knowledge and technology has not changed our nature. God makes a way to bring his creation into right relationship with himself again; one savior and one Lord.

WEEK 3

Reading 3

BIBLE STORY

Despite the tower of Babel and mankind's continuing struggle with evil, God continues the line of people calling on his name from Noah to Abram. God makes a great promise to Abram that changes all human history.

Genesis 11:27—12:9; 14:1-2, 10-24

Why does God start with one old man, Abram, instead of a great king with an army?

How is that like later when God sends his son Jesus to be born in a manger with the animals?

Why does Abram save his nephew Lot even though he does not approve of Lot's friends?

BIBLE CONVERSATION

The Bible says more about this mysterious character Melchizedek later.

Psalm 110, Hebrews 6:19—7:3

Melchizedek quickly appears and disappears from the story. Why is he so important?

Who does the Bible say he might be?

Why does God give us things we do not yet understand?

WEEK 3: READING 3

Leader Notes

After Adam and Noah, God again starts everything over with one person, Abram from Ur. God makes a promise that he will bring blessing into the world through this one man. Humans are judged by how we deal with Abram and his descendants. Eventually the culmination of that promise will be the Jewish Messiah, Jesus. It will be a long road with many twists and turns, but God keeps his promise.

Abram lives his life and makes decisions as we also must. Years go by with not much happening, and then, suddenly, amazing things happen. Abram's encounter with Melchizedek is mysterious and spoken about centuries later in the Psalms by David, then again centuries later in the New Testament. This meeting is a doorway to the heavenly places with eternal meaning and consequence. We expect that God will answer many of our questions. He will give us eyes to see things we cannot now perceive.

WEEK 4

Reading 1

BIBLE STORY

After Abram rescues Lot and gives a tenth of his possessions to Melchizedek, God expands and specifies his earlier promise to Abram. He promises Abram a nation-size family and a special land.

Genesis 15

What good things does God do when he puts first Adam (Genesis 2:21–22), and now Abram, to sleep?

What does it mean that Abram cannot promise anything back (because he is asleep) to the Lord when they make this deal (covenant)?

Should God be worried that he will still have to keep the promise, even if Abram fails?

BIBLE CONVERSATION

God is simply looking for Abram's complete trust and allegiance.

Romans 4:1–8

Does God choose Abram because Abram is great?

Or is Abram great because God chooses him?

How is our relationship with God the same as Abram's?

WEEK 4: READING 1

Leader Notes

Abram sets up a covenant ceremony with animal body parts on either side of a path as the Lord instructs. In the ceremony, the normal expectation is that they both walk the path between the animal halves. The covenant is normally a promise between two people with a guarantee like, "May I be like these dead animals if I break my part of the bargain." But in this covenant, the only one to walk through and make a promise is the Lord! He puts Abram to sleep. So, God is going to keep this promise regardless of what Abram does!

In Romans, Paul is explaining how our trust in Jesus is like Abram's trust in God. Paul quotes this passage from Genesis and the Psalms. Abram has already trusted God by moving to the land of Canaan. That is enough for God to seal the covenant with him.

WEEK 4

Reading 2

BIBLE STORY

God's promise of a son to Abram and Sarai is hard for them to imagine because they are long past childbearing years.

Genesis 16

How much trouble does Sarai and Abram's idea—to have a baby with Hagar—create?

Does God need an idea from us—like Sarai's—that seems more possible to us?

How should we use our great ideas in our life with God?

BIBLE CONVERSATION

Abram and Sarai try to help God, but he does not need help. His purposes are carried out with Abram's faith. Sarah and Hagar come to represent great truths for us to this day.

Galatians 4:21–31

Why do we strive so hard to impress God with how good we are?

What does he already know about us?

Why is it so hard for us to accept the freedom God has for us?

WEEK 4: READING 2

Leader Notes

Sarai is under a lot of social pressure. Often in that world, if a woman does not have a baby boy within ten years of marriage, her husband has the right to divorce her. Abram isn't like that, but she feels pressure because God is promising that a nation will come from Abram's body. God will further specify that the nation of people will come from Sarai's body as well. He will change Sarai's name to Sarah.

Paul uses Sarah and Hagar as an allegory many centuries later. It is not easy to understand, but important. We are made free by trusting God in Jesus. Then our good deeds are done like a child doing work at home just because he loves his family. If we try to get God to notice, or accept us because we are doing so many good things, we are like an employee; we get paid for our work and that is it. Paul makes Sarah and Hagar a picture of that.

WEEK 4

Reading 3

BIBLE STORY

Thirteen years after Ishmael is born, God speaks to Abram again and reaffirms the promise with new names and a sign, circumcision.

Genesis 17

Why does God give Abram and Sarai new names?

Why is Abraham laughing (Genesis 17:17)?

What do we hope for that seems impossible?

BIBLE CONVERSATION

God still asks that we trust and serve him, not knowing how everything will turn out.

Romans 4:16–25

How does God later include different families and tribes as Abraham's children (Romans 4:16, 23–25)?

Why is it good and right to trust God even when things seem difficult and impossible?

WEEK 4: READING 3

Leader Notes

After God says Abraham's heir will come also from Sarah's body, Abraham laughs and reminds God of his son Ishmael. God says to name this son Laughter (Isaac). God takes them to a seeming impossible place. Who could forget a son born to parents this old? What is at stake is the promise given to Abraham. In the realm of the impossible, God does not need our version of this (Ishmael), but since someone else is now involved, he will be greatly blessed as well.

Here circumcision is the defining covenant of belonging to Abraham. The event happens before the law, but it is written about after Moses has received the law. The writer knows what this will mean. Moses is confronted on his way to Egypt for not circumcising his sons. The generation that Moses addresses in Deuteronomy stops to catch up on all the missing circumcisions before they enter the land after more than four decades in the wilderness.

Abraham and Sarah are still the picture of trusting in God's impossible things we have not yet seen with our eyes. Abraham has already demonstrated his faith with actions by moving to the promised land. He is our picture as we pledge faith to our risen King Jesus whom we will see face to face. Those of us who are not Abraham's physical descendants (and not under the command to be physically circumcised) are participants in the same faith in the same King.

WEEK 5

Reading 1

BIBLE STORY

While Abraham is waiting for the promise to be fulfilled, God appears to him once more. God's promise is sure, and here it is contrasted with the pervasiveness of sin.

Genesis 18:1–22

Three men appear to Abraham (Genesis 18:2), but only two arrive in Sodom (Genesis 19:1). Who is the third that stays and keeps talking to Abraham (Genesis 18:22)?

What does it mean that God has wonderful plans for us (Genesis 18:17–19) at the same time he deals with the terrible things we do (Genesis 18:20–21)?

BIBLE CONVERSATION

Despite how pervasive sin and death are, like in Sodom, God makes a way for us.

Romans 5:6–8

How much does God love us?

How do we know that?

WEEK 5: READING 1

Leader Notes

Abraham with the Lord and two angels is an amazing scene. The Bible story is skillful. It starts by saying that Abraham sees three men but by the end the reader realizes who is there. This is a growing revelation for the reader, perhaps like Abraham experiences.

Abraham knows the Lord and so recognizes that these three are not just some guys. We can learn from that awareness as we know God better and better. The Lord reinforces his promise while he informs Abraham of the trouble his nephew Lot is in, again.

Sodom is a picture of God's saving power in the midst of his righteous judgment. Jesus the Messiah comes and drags us out of the Sodom we live in. He does so at great cost, his life.

WEEK 5

Reading 2

BIBLE STORY

Knowing Abraham's concern for his relative, God sends messengers to rescue Lot from the coming judgement.

Genesis 19:1–29

God uses Abraham to rescue Lot and the King of Sodom previously. Why is he destroying Sodom now?

Why is judgment God's business and not ours?

Why is it better to live in a tent with the Lord like Abraham than in a walled city away from the Lord, like Lot?

BIBLE CONVERSATION

God never changes his mind about sin, but he also provides a great life for us, if we choose.

Romans 6:22–23

What is the difference between wages and a gift (Romans 6:23)?

Why is a gift far better than wages, especially if God is giving it?

WEEK 5: READING 2

Leader Notes

All the theoretical questions about sin and judgment quickly blow away when we are confronted by the actual ugliness of the human heart acting out its base desires. Lot is a disturbing picture of how compromised we can become. He knows that leaving his guests in the town square will be a disaster, so he rightly brings them home. But then he offers his daughters to the mob to maintain his hospitality obligations to the special guests. Sin is a cruel master.

The outcry coming to the Lord (Genesis 19:13) is not from moral police; it is from victims of the violence and lust. Sin extracts a horrifying cost in human pain and misery. Those victims are often the next generation victimizing others. This is not primarily aimed at homosexuality but certainly takes in aspects of it, as mentioned in Romans 1. It is mainly about the corruption and violence mentioned a few chapters ago in Genesis 6.

We cannot say that God's laws do not apply to us because we are not as bad as others. We keep our eyes on God's standard of holiness and realize that we are all drowning in the same ocean of sin with no way out except through God's great gift of eternal life in Messiah Jesus.

WEEK 5

Reading 3

BIBLE STORY

The fulfillment of God's promise, Isaac, brings Abraham's greatest joy and his greatest test.

Genesis 21:1–8; 22:1–19

Why does Abraham give his son the name Laughter? Why is that funny?

What is hard to understand about God asking Abraham to sacrifice Isaac?

What is easy to understand about it?

BIBLE CONVERSATION

Trusting God to provide is, was, and always will be the path of life with him.

Romans 8:1, 15–17, 26–39

How much of life is hard to understand?

How does God help us with that (Romans 8:26–27, 38–39)?

WEEK 5: READING 3

Leader Notes

There is no internal dialogue in this Bible story. We do not know what Abraham is thinking. He is simply obeying. This does not fit well with other things God asks people to do in the Bible. It is incredibly ironic because it has been such a long time waiting for Isaac's birth. The New Testament gives a line of reasoning from Abraham's perspective at Hebrews 11:19.

We do not and will not completely get this, but it is important. It is a picture of a father sacrificing a son. Jesus as Son of God is sacrificed knowing that God will provide for the resurrection.

Romans 8 makes some amazing claims about God's love for us and our strong place in his spiritual realm because of our bond with Messiah Jesus.

WEEK 6

Reading 1

BIBLE STORY

God's promise continues from Abraham through Isaac, and then one of Isaac's sons.

Genesis 25:5–11, 19–34

Isaac's older brother Ishmael is an archer like Esau. Why does Isaac favor his son Esau (Genesis 25:27–28)?

What are Jacob and Esau's different relationships to their birthright? What does this tell us about them?

BIBLE CONVERSATION

God's right to make choices can be difficult for us to understand. Many centuries later, Paul uses the birth of Isaac, Jacob, and Esau to explore God's choices.

Romans 9:6–21

The Jacob and Esau story is ancient when Paul writes about it two thousand years ago in Romans. Why is it still important today?

Why does God choose things that seem unfair to us?

How is that different than when another person decides something that seems unfair to us?

WEEK 6: READING 1

Leader Notes

The twins Jacob and Esau are as different as can be. The culture is absolutely set that the oldest son inherits, even though the Bible story has plenty of younger brothers inheriting. With twins, the first to be born is it. The writer is clearly telling us that Esau is not qualified to inherit. He cares so little for his birthright that he trades it for some food. His *actions* trump whatever *feeling* he has about it.

Isaac is blind, and perhaps blind to what is going on. His blindness will be explored as the story goes on. He is going with the culture despite what the Lord said to his wife Rebekah.

Paul uses this story in Genesis to make a theological point that God has the right to choose whomever he likes. We could say Isaac has a different mother than Ishmael for a reason that Isaac inherits the birthright as youngest. Also, his mother was a wife and not a slave. But in the case of twins, how is it decided? Is God confined or constrained to go with the culture? Absolutely not. He chooses Jacob. The quote about hating Esau is poetic hyperbole (exaggeration to make a point) from the prophet Malachi; God actually blesses Esau. God hates Esau only in comparison to how much he loves Jacob. God is not unfair or unmerciful, but he has the right to decide and choose.

WEEK 6

Reading 2

BIBLE STORY

After selling his birthright, Esau still expects the blessing from Isaac. Rebekah and Jacob have a different plan.

Genesis 27:1—28:5

Isaac is physically blind, what else is he not seeing about his sons?

Why is Isaac easy to trick (Genesis 27:4, 22)? Does he know it is Jacob?

How do things we love make us blind sometimes?

BIBLE CONVERSATION

Later we are told plainly what is strongly implied earlier in Genesis.

Hebrews 12:14-17

We feel sorry for Esau because he is upset, but why do the Bible writers (in Genesis and Hebrews) not take his side?

If Jacob is supposed to get the blessing, does that make his deception okay?

How might God help Jacob work on his bad habits?

WEEK 6: READING 2

Leader Notes

There is a lot of tension in this story because Isaac, out of the blue, decides it is time to give the blessing to Esau. He says he might die soon, but in fact lives many more years. The story is well crafted and written to be read out loud, like most of the Bible.

This story is about God being persistent despite the dysfunction of his chosen family. The human impulse is to feel sorry for Esau being victimized, but the text is clear that he is not interested in or worthy of the blessing. He wants the benefits but is not suited or willing to carry the responsibilities. Jacob obtains the blessing by deception, which is wrong, but it is also testament to his cleverness, a trait esteemed by the Bible.

Dealing with the ambiguities in the Bible stories is like our everyday life. We make most decisions without having all the information we want or need. A big part of understanding comes from continuing to walk with God: watching, listening, learning.

Jacob's cleverness will be an issue his whole life. He will soon be outwitted by his clever uncle, then later by his own sons. Some of us are cleverer than others, but none of us outwit God. Manipulating others always comes back to bite us.

WEEK 6

Reading 3

BIBLE STORY

Running from his brother Esau, Jacob receives assurance from the Lord that he is indeed carrying the promise and will be brought back from exile.

Genesis 28:10–22

Jacob is in trouble for what he did. Why does God, at the same time, tell him that everything will be alright?

Why is Jacob negotiating, even though God is making a promise to him (Genesis 28:20–22)?

How long is God able to remember his promises? What are some things he promises us?

BIBLE CONVERSATION

The descendants of exiled Jacob are later reassured by the comforting promise of return from another exile.

Jeremiah 31:8–15

Why do some promises get fulfilled only after our lifetime?

Does that mean God does not love us?

What does it mean that God makes us part of something bigger than ourselves? What are some of those bigger things?

WEEK 6: READING 3

Leader Notes

God makes a promise to Jacob's grandfather Abraham, which is then passed to his son Isaac, and now to Jacob, who is running for his life. He is exiled, but the blessing has passed to him. In this amazing scene God himself appears to Jacob and assures him that he is the chosen one. Jacob is in trouble for what he did, but he is loved and blessed. It will be twenty years before he returns with his wives and children, but God is with him. Jacob is fleeing in fright. He is rightly afraid of what is behind him and of what is ahead. He is in survival mode, so he tries to negotiate with God for what he needs. God already knows what he needs, but Jacob must live through the trouble he himself has created. He knows that what he is seeing is amazing but is unable to process it yet fully.

Generations and centuries later Jeremiah speaks to Jacob's children that are now the nation of Israel. They are going into exile for their sins like Jacob. They are still loved and blessed, but in terrible trouble of their own making. God again reassures them that their children and grandchildren will come back and live in Abraham's blessing. Verse 15 is about the city of Ramah, which is the deportation point where the Babylonians are separating parents from the young people they are taking to Babylon. Daniel is probably one of those taken away at perhaps fifteen years old and never seen again by his family. This verse is later quoted at Matthew 2:18 to describe the sorrow when Herod murders the baby boys of Bethlehem in his attempt to kill the baby Jesus. That young family goes into exile to Egypt to survive and come back later.

WEEK 7

Reading 1

BIBLE STORY

Jacob's exile begins with an introduction to a bigger deceiver than himself. Like blind Isaac, Jacob is fooled in a tent, in the dark, following senses other than hearing and seeing.

Genesis 29:1–30

What are some things Jacob probably learns in those fourteen years working out in the hot sun and freezing nights?

Why does God do things slower than we want many times?

How do we really learn to trust God in life?

BIBLE CONVERSATION

Beyond our own cleverness and struggle, God says again and always, "trust me."

Romans 10:8–11

How many people live and die between the time of Jacob and Jesus—perhaps two thousand years—waiting to see where God is taking all of this?

Why is making Jesus our Lord and living for him so important?

It sounds simple but is it easy? Why?

WEEK 7: READING 1

Leader Notes

Jacob is in trouble, alone in a strange place hundreds of miles from home. He is in trouble for cleverly deceiving his brother. He is unable to access any of the wealth with which he has been blessed. He must work hard for whatever he gets.

What he wants is this beautiful girl, Rachel. Laban takes advantage of Jacob's desires like Jacob took advantage of Isaac's desires to steal the blessing from Esau. We, as readers, have a laugh at Jacob's expense. It is a comedy scene that will produce a big family, but Jacob is still struggling to trust that the Lord loves and cares for him.

We still struggle with those same trust issues. One of Jacob's descendants, Jesus, becomes the object of trust and allegiance in God's salvation for all humanity.

WEEK 7

Reading 2

BIBLE STORY

After twenty long years away, Jacob heads home to face his deepest fears; the truth about himself, his brother, and his God.

Genesis 32

The Lord tells Jacob to go home and sends angels to greet him. Why is he still afraid?

Why does God make Jacob fight to get back home?

Would God make us struggle to do the right thing?

BIBLE CONVERSATION

God does not reject Jacob then and does not reject Jacob's people now.

Romans 11:1–6

How is your life story different than anyone else's?

How can Jesus be the central place that all of God's plans come together for Jewish and gentile people, that is, everyone?

WEEK 7: READING 2

Leader Notes

Angels greet Jacob coming home like he had seen them when he was leaving. Ages before, Adam and Eve are kept away from the garden and the Tree of Life by angels. Centuries later, Joshua meets an angel coming back into this place. This raises the possibility that this land of Canaan is where the garden was. The Bible does not answer the question, but the next place we see the Tree of Life from the garden is in the New Jerusalem in the book of Revelation.

Jacob has learned great things about God in twenty years of exile, but now he must protect his family. He is terrified. He is facing Esau's four hundred-man army with only his wits and the hope of God's protection.

Before he meets his brother, the Lord wrestles with Jacob as he reenters the land. Jacob must fight for it. It is terrifying, but Jacob knows that God is right in the middle of the whole thing. If he survives his contest with God himself, he will perhaps survive Esau. The story keeps us on edge, like all good stories.

In Romans, Paul assures the Jewish and gentile followers of Jesus that Jacob's story and his blessing from Abraham are alive and active to this day. He reminds them of the long-after-Jacob story of Elijah running for his life. God assures Elijah that all is not lost when we live in the promise that God never fails to keep. Even when all the nation of Israel does not receive their Messiah, Jesus, some do, and God is happy to work with that little group. That little group from the big one is called in the Bible a "remnant."

WEEK 7

Reading 3

BIBLE STORY

After wrestling with God, Jacob goes out to meet Esau.

Genesis 33

Why is the order in which Jacob puts the wives and children to face danger important to their ongoing relationships with each other, especially with Joseph?

Why is imagining our fears often worse than they turn out to be?

Why does God want us to fear only him?

BIBLE CONVERSATION

Whatever else happens along the way, it is our faith in God that he honors and remembers.

Hebrews 11:17–20

Why do we have to make decisions every day without knowing what will happen?

Might God still bless us if we make a mistake in one of our decisions?

WEEK 7: READING 3

Leader Notes

Jacob has the courage to be out in front to meet Esau, but he tips his hand about who he loves most by the order in which he places the wives with their children. This creates resentment that shows up years later when the sons of Jacob's concubines sell their half-brother Joseph into slavery.

The meeting with Esau goes well, but Jacob politely makes a promise he has no intention of keeping; he is never going to Seir, where his brother lives outside the land. Jacob reenters the land he is inheriting carrying a lot of the same baggage he left with twenty years earlier. But he has obeyed God and is where he is supposed to be.

Jacob's test is hard, like his grandfather Abraham's test of offering up Isaac. The nature of God is demonstrated in that he blesses both Jacob and Esau, even as he had blessed both Isaac and Ishmael. He is a giver of gifts.

WEEK 8

Reading 1

BIBLE STORY

After Jacob faces his fears, God again appears to him.

Genesis 35

Why do we need to eat and sleep every day?

Why do we also need reminding of who God is and what he is doing (Genesis 35:9–15)?

Why are the twelve sons of Jacob, also called Israel, important?

Jacob and Esau together bury their father, Isaac. How is God able to bring everything around that seems forever broken?

BIBLE CONVERSATION

God's promise to Jacob stands to this day.

Romans 11:25–36

If we say or think, "God loves me more than you," why is that conceited, arrogant, and wrong (Romans 11:25)?

If a mystery is something we do not understand, is it something God does not understand?

Why is it good for us to live with mysteries? How does it help us be less conceited?

WEEK 8: READING 1

Leader Notes

After all the craziness of getting back into the land and meeting Esau, Jacob has to leave behind the baggage of the pagan world. God brings him back to the place he fled from Esau and blesses him again. The ongoing promise is strong despite the ups, downs, and difficulties of Jacob's life.

Long later Paul reminds us that God keeps his promises, even in dealing with those who reject him. He assures the gentiles in the church at Rome that God is not yet finished with the children of Jacob, even the ones who rejected their Messiah. We should not be arrogant toward them or gloat, but rather stand in grateful awe at the mystery of God revealed in Messiah Jesus. The church did not listen to Paul's words and had a disgraceful relationship with the Jewish community for many centuries, culminating in the holocaust of World War II. We now must walk Paul's tightrope of loving while disagreeing.

WEEK 8

Reading 2

BIBLE STORY

After the death of Isaac, Jacob's later life is filled with trouble caused by his own sons.

Genesis 37

Why are Ruben and Judah trying to save Joseph?

How is God going to keep his original promise to their father Abraham that he would have a big, amazing family? Does that mean no problems?

Why are these troubles coming to haunt Jacob after he finally starts doing the right things?

Why do we feel strongly about the way our brothers and sisters treat us?

BIBLE CONVERSATION

Despite Jacob's troubles, God insists that he act worthy of the promise, and he insists that we do the same.

Romans 12:1–2

How does Jesus make it possible to be part of God's big, amazing family in this world?

What does it mean to wake up every day and be a living sacrifice for God?

Is living every day for the Lord harder than dying for him once? Why?

WEEK 8: READING 2

Leader Notes

All of Jacob's manipulations come rolling back over him like a wave. He creates a lot of resentment between his sons over the years by showing blatant favoritism. He also does not deal directly with wrong actions like Ruben sleeping with his concubine and Simeon and Levi murdering the men of Shechem.

Jacob the deceiver is once again deceived, this time by his sons. This lie about the fate of Joseph—killed by wild animals—becomes a huge factor in the ongoing relationship Jacob has with his sons. They all know what happened, except perhaps Benjamin. They are living a lie for many years as adults while raising their own families. Family dysfunction rolls from one generation to the next. One of our great roles in life is to stop this cycle by doing the right thing with our own family even, especially, if we did not learn good habits from the family into which we were born. This classic Bible story shows God always leading us to do the right thing in the midst of no-win situations. It is about trusting God to bring our life to good places.

In Jesus, we are called not just to give up our life for him, but rather to live for him every day. A sacrifice dies once, but a living sacrifice gives over its life every day. That is what God is asking of his children.

WEEK 8

Reading 3

BIBLE STORY

Joseph's brothers sell him into slavery, where his goodness gets him in and out of trouble.

Genesis 39

How does Joseph's good character get him into trouble?

How does his good character bring God's blessing to all those around him?

How does God bring blessing into our difficult circumstances with our good behavior?

BIBLE CONVERSATION

Whatever circumstance we find ourselves in, we are to be about the business that God has for us.

Romans 12:3–8

What are some of the gifts God gives us as followers of Jesus?

How should we use them?

How does God change the world by us using our gifts?

WEEK 8: READING 3

Leader Notes

Joseph's lack of tact with his brothers gets him to Egypt. Now his refusal to do wrong things gets him in prison. But his goodness, while annoying, also blesses those around him, which gives God opportunity to spread the blessing further and further. This does not mean things quickly get better for Joseph or us. God wants us to know that in doing right we are showing his love and truth no matter what. He is happy to change the world with that. How many good decisions have been made through thousands of years because of young people reading Joseph's story?

Our life in Jesus is meant to be strengthened by each of us using what the Lord has given us for the benefit of one another. We bless others and we in turn are blessed. The gifts given by the Spirit are designed to help one another. The list of gifts in Romans is only partial; there are other spiritual gifts in the New Testament. They are not for being or acting alone. He makes us dependent on one another as God blesses the world through us. We might be forced to act alone, like Joseph, but God wants us together, like Joseph should have been with his family.

WEEK 9

Reading 1

BIBLE STORY

Joseph has been thrown into Pharaoh's dungeon and forgotten by everyone, except God.

Genesis 41:1–46

Does Joseph know what good things will eventually happen by doing the right thing in each bad situation?

Joseph has been in Egypt thirteen years before he works for Pharaoh. Why does God want us to do the right thing even if we never become important or famous?

What will your life be like in thirteen years? How old will you be? What will be different then?

BIBLE CONVERSATION

Whether in a dungeon or in Pharaoh's court, our behavior should reflect who God is.

Romans 12:9–13

How are these things easier to do on good days and harder on bad days?

How are Joseph's good decisions affecting us still today?

Will God make our good decisions today affect people a long time from now? How?

WEEK 9: READING 1

Leader Notes

Joseph is born to a wealthy father who dotes on him. He spends the last part of his teens and all of his twenties as a slave. Is God unfair? Does God owe us a particular life? Joseph struggles, stubbornly does the right thing, and God blesses him. God asks the same of his children still. We get to be in the story God writes for us. The New Testament message for followers of Jesus still upholds Joseph's right behavior and decisions.

WEEK 9

Reading 2

BIBLE STORY

When Joseph is working for Pharaoh, there is a famine and all his brothers come to Egypt for food. They do not recognize Joseph, who is now the governor.

Genesis 45:1—46:7

Why does Joseph not take revenge on his brothers for selling him into slavery?

How is God's promise to Abraham—"I will make you great and bless the world through you"—working out in the crazy hard circumstances of this story?

BIBLE CONVERSATION

Joseph is a great example of letting God take up our cause. Following Jesus is still about doing exactly that.

Romans 12:14–21

Paul is quoting Jesus, the Proverbs, and the Law of Moses. Why is it important that God has been doing the same thing all along?

Does this mean that we must like or trust bad people?

How do we live bigger and better than revenge? Why?

WEEK 9: READING 2

Leader Notes

Joseph's brothers are driven to Egypt by the famine. Their wealth is in sheep. They need food for the animals, their servants and themselves. There are echoes of the Abraham story here. Abraham was driven by famine to Egypt as well. The Nile River provided water when everywhere else was in a drought.

God's people often develop character in hard times. When the hard times are from people persecuting us, we can get stuck living in the past if we are living on revenge. Joseph's willingness to see God's hand in his life is the same lesson we learn as the people of Jesus.

The New Testament continues with Joseph's same principles of godliness. We are now empowered by the Holy Spirit through Jesus for this, even if we are not as gifted or strong as Joseph.

WEEK 9

Reading 3

BIBLE STORY

Jacob speaks of "the last days" as he blesses his sons and dies in Egypt. Fourth son Judah is blessed as ruler and Joseph is rewarded with a double portion for his faithfulness. The coming king will be from Judah's tribe.

Genesis 49:1–10, 22–33

Why is having children such an amazing blessing all through the rest of our life?

Why does Jacob want to be buried back in Canaan?

Jesus is the King from the tribe of Judah, the Lion of Judah. How do we show that he is our king?

BIBLE CONVERSATION

The coming of Jesus does not erase promises and inheritance, it multiplies them. Our response to God's generous gifts is more generosity and giving.

Romans 15:23–27

Why are followers of Jesus everywhere responsible for one another?

Why does God give all of us different gifts?

Why is following Jesus so deeply tied to Israel and the Jewish people?

WEEK 9: READING 3

Leader Notes

To raise children from birth is to really know them. We know what is behind their behavior as adults. Their children, our grandchildren, can be a redemption for the many mistakes we make on our journey through life. To be surrounded by our children is a great blessing from God.

Jacob understands that it will be easy to get forever stuck in Egypt, but the promise to his grandfather Abraham is tied to the land of Canaan. Jacob insists on being buried there. That gives his descendants one more reason to leave Egypt and come back to the land.

These blessings of family now stretch over all the world for followers of Jesus. But Paul insists that we stay oriented still to the promise, people, and place where everything started.

WEEK 10

Reading 1

BIBLE STORY

When Jacob and all his sons go down to Egypt, they stay for a long time. God finally raises up a baby who will bring his people home.

Exodus 1–2:10

Even though life in Egypt becomes hard for Israel, how is God keeping his promise to Abraham (Exodus 1:7)?

Baby Moses is placed in a basket called an ark, like Noah's ark. How is the basket like the ark?

What king is trying to kill baby Jesus a long time later (Matthew 2:13–14)?

How are those two kings alike? How are those two babies alike?

BIBLE CONVERSATION

God continues to raise up things, like helpless babies, that seem to us weak and unimportant, to accomplish his work.

1 Corinthians 1:18–25

Why are most people ready to follow a handsome king on a horse and with an army?

Why does God often use regular-looking people to change the world?

Can God change the world with any of us?

WEEK 10: READING 1

Leader Notes

Seventy of Jacob's descendants go down to Egypt, and after four centuries they are a great nation. This is a fulfillment of God's original promise to Abraham. The blessings continue down to the people of Jesus, Jew and gentile, but it already reaches a fulfillment in Egypt.

Pharaoh killing babies is echoed long later when Herod does the same thing trying to destroy baby Jesus, the King of the Jews. The weakness of babies is a way that God shows himself behind stories all through the Bible. Moses and Jesus are the two biggest examples. God shows himself strong in our weakness.

Paul points this out to the Corinthians long later. They wanted to show their status over one another. Paul reminds them that God always starts with weak but willing servants.

WEEK 10

Reading 2

BIBLE STORY

Moses is raised forty years in Pharaoh's court and then flees for his life after killing an Egyptian. He goes to the desert of Sinai and lives forty more years. Finally, it is time.

Exodus 2:23—3:22

Why is it hard to wait and see what God will do next?

Why is God okay with the things we are not good at (Exodus 3:11–12)?

BIBLE CONVERSATION

When Moses loses everything, he is ready for the mission God has for him.

1 Corinthians 1:26–31

Why is this not an excuse to be lazy by saying, "Well, there is nothing I can do"?

To "boast in the Lord," why is it important to first do everything possible and still need help?

WEEK 10: READING 2

Leader Notes

Moses lives forty years in Pharaoh's court, flees for his life, and lives another forty years in the wilderness. God speaks to him when he is eighty—a long time to wait. Moses will live another forty years leading the Israelites through the wilderness after bringing them out of Egypt and giving them the law.

God's *modus operandi* is to use unexpected people so that all will know it is the Lord bringing this thing about. It runs counter to human nature. We can be tempted to do less than we are capable of and say that the Lord will make up the difference, but that is wrong. That is putting God to the test, asking him to do what we are too lazy to do for ourselves.

We ought to study, work, and throw ourselves into what is before us and know that God will take that and make more of it than we are able. Joseph and Daniel are great examples of this truth. It is only when we have done all we can that we understand how weak we are and what God has done for us.

WEEK 10

Reading 3

BIBLE STORY

Back in Egypt, after God brings nine plagues, Pharaoh stubbornly refuses to let Moses lead his people out to the desert of Sinai.

Exodus 11

In the Bible, what does it mean to believe in God?

If we say that we believe in God, but act like we do not believe in him, what does that mean?

If we think we are stronger than God, do we really believe in him?

BIBLE CONVERSATION

Part of believing in God is knowing we will someday meet him. Pharaoh chooses to meet God as his judge. We can meet God as our heavenly father.

1 Corinthians 3:10–15

If we do something wrong, would we rather talk to the police or our parents about it?

What is the difference between meeting God as judge or as heavenly father?

How can we have God as our heavenly father instead of our judge?

WEEK 10: READING 3

Leader Notes

The Bible has a far deeper notion of believing than simple mental assent. "Sure, I guess so" will not do. If we believe in God, we live for him. He is so great that there is no other option. If we believe that Jesus is the Messiah—that is, the Anointed King of Kings—he is so great that we have no other option than to serve him. Saying we believe him without serving him will not fool him even if everyone else (including ourselves) is fooled.

Paul, in Romans 9:16–18, uses Pharaoh as an example of God's right to harden someone's heart or save them. It is not an easy or quickly solvable topic. If God hardens Pharaoh, why is Pharaoh at fault? Later, he encourages the Romans to believe, that is, to choose and do what is right. So, God chooses, and we choose as well; a mystery. We grapple with this topic, but ultimately we live with it rather than completely understanding it.

In 1 Corinthians 3 Paul speaks of our works being tested. It is a kind of judgment, but one within a context. Our souls are already saved, that is, God's judgment of our very souls is already decided because of the shed blood of Jesus by which we are made righteous. So, as our father rather than judge, God is telling us what all our efforts meant. Did we do everything for money and fame, or did we serve the Lord with an upright heart?

WEEK 11

Reading 1

BIBLE STORY

God prepares to strike the Egyptians with a final, tenth plague. He tells Moses and Aaron what to do and what this will mean for them in all the years ahead.

Exodus 12:1–28

This Passover sacrifice is to be done by every family—why is home the place where everything starts?

Why is the blood of the Passover lamb so important for getting Israel out of slavery?

Why is listening and obeying so important in this first Passover?

BIBLE CONVERSATION

The first gentile followers of Jesus know about and celebrate the Passover. By this they understand that Jesus is the sacrifice that works for everyone, forever. God's work in the Passover continues saving his people.

1 Corinthians 5:6–8

Leaven is like sin—why do we have to get it away from ourselves?

When we take communion, how is it a reminder of the Passover?

How is sin—doing only what we want—the biggest kind of slavery for all people?

WEEK 11: READING 1

Leader Notes

Israel painting the blood of the Passover lamb on their door frames in Egypt is an act of faith. The Israelites obey, trusting that God will do what he says. This is centered in the family home and around the table. Everyone is included under the blood, even if they do not have a family, even if they are Egyptians or other foreigners.

This blood is a shield against the coming judgment of God. God is settling accounts with Pharaoh. God's people simply need to trust and obey him. Those concepts are central to the New Testament and the gospel.

Paul uses the Passover as an illustration that the Corinthian gentile believers obviously understand and practice. It is the center of the fulfillment of God's redemption from the bondage of sin. Jewish believers today have reintroduced the practice of "keeping the festival" as Paul says here. Celebrating the Passover of Jesus is a deeply instructive practice for teaching the Bible and its theology to children as well as adults.

WEEK 11

Reading 2

BIBLE STORY

The Israelites are prepared for the Passover. When they are finally set free, they are beginning a whole new life, a new journey.

Exodus 12:29–42

How hard would it be to move after our family lived somewhere for 430 years?

How hard would it be to start on a journey, moving to a place we have never seen?

Why does God take us to new places and out of old places?

BIBLE CONVERSATION

The freedom of the ancient Passover has become the freedom of the Passover Lamb, Jesus. It is freedom we share with others. Following Jesus is moving from old places to new ones where he takes us.

1 Corinthians 9:19–27

If we want others to be part of God's family, why do we start where their life is?

How different is following Jesus than going to church and then doing whatever I want?

How do we learn to be on this journey through life with Jesus?

WEEK 11: READING 2

Leader Notes

The first Passover is different than all the ones that come after. The first is eaten while prepared to travel. All after are as free people at leisure.

The Israelites learn more from the plagues than Pharaoh and the Egyptians. By the last plague, the Israelites believe enough to obey and get under the protection of the blood of the Passover lamb. This is not easy. Some stranger comes and says to revolt and follow him to a place where our family left 430 years ago; what do we do?

The Passover is the Bible's foundation for understanding God's redemption from slavery. At the Last Supper, Jesus is God redeeming his people—all who will come—from humanity's complete slavery to sin.

Being under the blood of the Passover lamb and walking through the Red Sea are done by faith. Following Jesus out of slavery to sin, by his blood, and through whatever is next, is done by faith. What does that look like? It is different for everyone, but God demands that we start walking and trusting that he is taking us where he wants us.

We do for others what God does for us. We go where they are, like he comes to us. We love because Jesus loves us.

WEEK 11

Reading 3

BIBLE STORY

After the tenth plague, the Israelites are sent out of Egypt. They walk through the sea on dry ground, by faith.

Exodus 14

When the Israelites are trapped against the sea they scream in terror (Exodus 14:10–12). Why would we probably do the same thing?

Have you ever come close to dying? How do you remember it?

What has happened in your life that makes you trust the Lord?

BIBLE CONVERSATION

The Israelites experience a salvation—a saving—from Egypt that is still a picture and an example for us.

1 Corinthians 10:1–12

Why is the whole Bible story important to know and understand?

Why is what we do today important in our whole life with Jesus?

WEEK 11: READING 3

Leader Notes

In the Bible, wine is a symbol of joy. Part of the Passover celebration is expressing sadness for what our enemies suffer. We remove a drop of wine (that is, joy) from our cup for each of the ten plagues against Egypt. Seeing our enemies suffer is not a cause for joy or celebration. Gloating is ungodly. We are sad for suffering, even when it is deserved. It does not have to be this way. We wish that everyone would find the joy of trusting and obeying the Lord.

The Israelites have been slaves for over four centuries. Being free is terrifying for many just released from bondage. The first generation coming out of Egypt sees amazing things with their own eyes, but they struggle to trust God. A big theme through the whole Bible, especially the Gospels, is that seeing miracles does not necessarily make people believe.

Israel's failure to trust the Lord in the wilderness becomes an example to us. Instead of gloating or being superior, we should see that our own position is perilous because we know much more than they did then. Because we know about the salvation of Jesus, we are liable for it, as the New Testament tells us in Hebrews 2:1–4.

WEEK 12

Reading 1

BIBLE STORY

The Israelites pass through the Red Sea and prepare themselves to meet with God.

Exodus 19

In keeping his promise to Abraham, what does God have in mind for Abraham's now-huge family (Exodus 19:3–8)?

If we heard the voice of God himself, would we always know he was real and do the right thing (Exodus 19:9)? How could the answer be no?

Why is there such distance between God and the people at Mt. Sinai?

BIBLE CONVERSATION

The Apostle Paul later explains why God gives the law to Israel. It is to keep Israel from being overcome by sin until the promised seed of Abraham—Jesus the Messiah—comes.

Galatians 3:19–27

Why are rules important, even if they are not everything?

Do we have rules at home? Why?

When we grow up, will we still have all the same rules?

How might they be different than the ones we have now?

WEEK 12: READING 1

Leader Notes

God wants the Israelites to have in their memories that they all heard his voice speaking the Ten Commandments. The assumption is that hearing God himself and seeing his power will keep people from sinning. That will not turn out to be so. However, God gives them the opportunity to hear him, and they must choose whether to obey. They agree to do whatever God says even before they hear, because God brought them out of slavery. They have another chance to agree after God speaks. They agree to the covenant, and then immediately break it.

This is a critical concept in the Bible. The law is related to the promise like childhood house rules are to growing up. The rules keep us from destroying ourselves and others until we are ready to see who we are and what life is about. The rules do not become wrong or even irrelevant; they are always taking us somewhere. We find that as we become mature, we live by those rules because that is how life is lived rightly and well.

WEEK 12

Reading 2

BIBLE STORY

The Israelites at the foot of Mt. Sinai are ready to hear from the God who brought them out of Egypt. He speaks what they, and we, need to hear.

Exodus 20:1–21

Why is honoring God important?

Why is honoring our parents important?

Why does God care so much about the way we treat one another?

BIBLE CONVERSATION

What the law terrifies Israel into doing we are to do in Messiah Jesus because we are free and empowered by the Spirit of God.

Galatians 5:13–26

What struggle are we in with ourselves?

How are the law and the Spirit trying to help us in our struggle with ourselves?

What things are we learning to do with God's help? Are we being more like him?

WEEK 12: READING 2

Leader Notes

The Ten Commandments are the basis of Western law systems, especially in the English-speaking world. There are four commandments about our relationship with God, one about our relationship with our parents, and five about our relationship with other people.

These commandments have all been broken in the Bible stories leading up to this chapter; even the Sabbath is broken on the journey from Egypt. The Law is a response to what people are already doing, not a theoretical idea about what they might do.

What the Law could not terrify us into doing, God now empowers us to do. Jesus comes as the new and better Moses. The Sermon on the Mount is a reminder of the scene at Mt. Sinai. God takes on flesh this time and talks to us, as one of us. Beyond not murdering, stealing, and envying, we are entering into love, joy, peace, and much more. We enter these things because we are born again and imbued with the very Spirit of God. We know that it looks like our living example, King Jesus.

WEEK 12

Reading 3

BIBLE STORY

After receiving the Ten Commandments, Israel agrees to live by this law, and they eat lunch with God to seal the deal.

Exodus 24

If we agree to do something, how important is it that we keep our promise?

If we saw God himself, how long would we remember it?

Why is God insistent on writing this agreement down (Exodus 24:7, 12)?

BIBLE CONVERSATION

The words from God at Sinai are a preparation for even more amazing things to come.

Hebrews 1:1–3; 2:1–4

The laws given are given at Sinai to prepare Israel to meet someone . . . Who?

If meeting with God at Sinai is a big deal, how important is meeting his Son, King Jesus?

Why do we make so many things more important than meeting the Lord?

WEEK 12: READING 3

Leader Notes

The laws given in Exodus 20–23 and 25–31 are the whole original law covenant, fairly short and simple. Everyone agrees to it and that should be that, but Israel breaks the covenant immediately in a big way with the golden calf.

God is very clear on all this, and the covenant should be doable, but the law is already having its peculiar effect on the nature of humans. This is nothing particular about the Israelites; it is a problem deeply resident in all people. The Israelites are chosen to display the effect of living under law.

God's Son comes and provides a way out of our inability to be godly. This is extremely personal and costly for God. He redeems us, that is, he buys us back out of the slavery we sold ourselves into. That is a final transaction, and we all respond in one way or another. If the penalties for ignoring the law were great, the penalty for ignoring the Son far more.

WEEK 13

Reading 1

BIBLE STORY

While Moses is on the mountain with God, the law is beginning to have its peculiar effect on the people.

Exodus 32

What important thing keeps the Lord from destroying Israel when they break the covenant of the law (Exodus 32:13–14)?

Everyone commits sins, but some people are committed to sinning. What is the difference?

Why do we want to be in the book that the Lord has written (Exodus 32:32)?

BIBLE CONVERSATION

The Law magnifies the truth about our fallen nature and, therefore, our need for a savior. Jesus is the fulfillment of everything the Lord starts with Moses, and much more.

Hebrews 3:1–6

Why are we so blessed by Moses?

Why are we far more blessed by Jesus?

WEEK 13: READING 1

Leader Notes

The golden calf is a big milestone in the Bible story. Everything looks great when Moses heads up the mountain to receive the stone tablets on which God writes the Ten Commandments. After the golden calf, God distances himself from the people so that he will not break out against them when they act this way again. He knows they will, like we all do. God also begins to add volumes to the Law, because they refuse to live by the intent of the law, which is to love God and one another.

The Lord's offer to Moses to destroy Israel and start over with him is a real offer but also a test. Moses acts as a mediator on behalf of his people, with whom he is also angry. He is a picture of the coming Jesus acting on our behalf in an even bigger way than Moses. Who Jesus is in relationship to Moses is one of the biggest questions in the New Testament.

Moses points to Jesus. He already knows that the law is a failure at bringing people to a living relationship with the Lord. The law's function will be to keep the people promised to Abraham, Isaac, and Jacob distinct from the world around them until Jesus is born to them.

WEEK 13

Reading 2

BIBLE STORY

After the golden calf, God continues to emphasize how serious the sin problem is. The sin problem is so serious that it involves shedding blood.

Leviticus 16; 17:10–14

Why do we need to stay in a good relationship with God?

Why do we need someone to act on our behalf so we can be close to God?

Since he created them, does God really want all those animals to die?

BIBLE CONVERSATION

After many centuries of priests sacrificing animals, Jesus the Messiah is now both high priest and sacrifice for those who trust him.

Hebrews 9:11–14, 23–28

What important things are happening in heaven as Jesus dies for us (Hebrews 9:24–26)?

When the gospel of Jesus goes out, why do so many priests respond to the sacrifice of Jesus (Acts 6:7)?

What should we do about the fact that Jesus died for our sins?

WEEK 13: READING 2

Leader Notes

Aaron, Moses' brother, is the first high priest and all high priests after are going to be from his sons. God does not immediately execute judgment on Aaron for making the golden calf. He obviously "has it coming." Other people die for that sin, but not Aaron. The issue is unresolved for the reader until Leviticus 10, when the sons of Aaron disobey the Lord's specific instructions and he kills them outright. They are the living expression of Aaron's big character flaw. God is not kidding about holiness and sin.

The constant, continual blood sacrifices are a reminder that the constant, continual sin of Israel and the world is life-and-death business. God is the source of all life and will not compromise with the corruption, violence, and death that has invaded his creation.

The high priest acts once a year on behalf of all Israel on Yom Kippur—the Day of Atonement—so that their sins will be accounted for and they can keep up accounts with God. There are many other sacrifices made for other reasons, but that is the most important one. Jesus steps in as the high priest who is also the sacrifice for everyone who comes to God through him.

WEEK 13

Reading 3

BIBLE STORY

Equipped with instructions on how to worship God, the Israelites are given a preview of the land God is giving to them.

Numbers 13:1–3, 21–33

Why is it important that the spies who go are Israel's leaders (Numbers 13:1–3)?

Why is it tragic that the people who are leaders are afraid?

If God destroys the Egyptian army, why will he have trouble taking Israel into the land?

BIBLE CONVERSATION

Centuries later the psalmist reminds us that the God who brings Israel out of Egypt and through the Red Sea can bring us to his resting place.

Psalm 95

Is it possible that our decisions today will become an example to others later?

Why is God counting on us to be good examples by doing what is right and courageous?

Does this mean we can do anything we think is right, or is God part of how we decide?

WEEK 13: READING 3

Leader Notes

After the golden calf, the next milestone failure for Israel is refusing to enter the land. This is the whole point of coming out of Egypt. The Lord has Moses send a leader from each tribe to be a spy. They should be the most capable, courageous, and visionary people in the entire nation; they are not. They are apparently the privileged from each tribe with the most to lose. They act in fear when they have every reason to lead where the Lord is showing them.

The Lord gives us every reason to be bold. He comes from heaven, lives as one of us, and dies for us. He gives us everything of real value in all the realms of heaven: salvation, love, grace, truth, and on and on.

If we have the privilege of leading, God holds us more responsible than those being led. We must live up to his calling. We will have failures, absolutely, but there are some tests we need to be ready to meet. The first and biggest test for all of us is to enter the Lord's rest. The only way in is through Jesus the Messiah.

WEEK 14

Reading 1

BIBLE STORY

When the leaders return from spying out the land, two say, "Let's go," and ten say, "It's too dangerous." The people must decide whether to be brave.

Numbers 14:1–35

Why does God get angry when the Israelites will not enter the land (Numbers 14:11, 20–23, 31–33)?

Is it fair that God holds us responsible for the choices we make in life?

How do we stay with God through the difficult decisions in life (Numbers 14:24, 30)?

BIBLE CONVERSATION

Now as then, the choice to move forward is ours, but we ignore God at our own risk.

Hebrews 3:16—4:2, 9–13

How do we now enter God's promise, his rest?

Why is it important that going to a new place means no longer being in the old place?

How is Jesus a new place for anyone who enters?

Leader Notes

Each generation chooses for themselves. This is a huge principle in the whole Bible. To use our children's safety as an excuse for ignoring God will not do; he will not accept it from us. Our children get dragged along through our foolishness and eventually must decide for themselves.

The writer of Hebrews in the New Testament uses Psalm 95, which uses Numbers 14, as a warning against failure to enter God's rest. The message echoes from the beginning to the end of the Bible. The ultimate form of entering God's rest is to enter his kingdom through his Son Jesus. We are all being challenged to trust the great things God has already done for us and take the risk of entering completely in, no turning back.

WEEK 14

Reading 2

BIBLE STORY

The older Israelites, after failing to enter the land, wander in the desert until they die. Moses now instructs the younger generation that will enter after their parents' refusal. He knows that the law is not going to keep them walking with God.

Deuteronomy 30:11–20; 31:1–13, 24–29

Why is it scary when someone new is in charge?

Why is the law so important, even though people find it impossible to follow?

How does God provide for us when things seem impossible?

BIBLE CONVERSATION

Moses knows that they will not keep the law, but that God will eventually fulfill his ancient promise to Abraham through a new covenant. This new covenant is foretold long after Moses by the prophet Jeremiah, quoted here, even later, by the writer of Hebrews.

Hebrews 8:7–12

Because Jesus is the new covenant, why are we so fortunate and blessed to know him?

How great is it to know and do the right thing?

What does it mean that God will forgive us and remember our sins no more?

WEEK 14: READING 2

Leader Notes

The book of Deuteronomy is Moses' message to the new generation, those under twenty years old when they walked through the Red Sea. They are now forty years older and must follow Joshua into the land.

Moses has watched how impossible it is to live by the law for forty years wandering in the wilderness. He knows they must live by the law—it should not be impossible—but they won't. It is a human problem. Moses writes down Genesis through Deuteronomy. He knows that Adam and Eve cannot not obey one simple rule, humanity cannot obey the few simple rules God gives Noah, and Israel will not live by the law.

We need a new covenant that we can live by and obey. That will come through Jesus the Messiah. The law is completely right and righteous and clearly points out our sin nature. But we need a new heart; we need to be born again.

WEEK 14

Reading 3

BIBLE STORY

In the Law, Moses tells us about the seed of the woman, the seed of Abraham, a king from Judah coming out of Egypt, and now a prophet like Moses. Could these all be the same person?

Deuteronomy 18:14–18; 34

How is Moses greater than the other prophets in the Bible (Deuteronomy 34:10–12)?

Why will it be such a long time (centuries) from Moses until Jesus comes?

If God gives us every good thing all at once, why do we stop appreciating how great it is?

BIBLE CONVERSATION

Long later, in Jesus' time, they are still looking for the prophet like Moses. They, like us, desperately need him.

John 1:19–21; 6:14–15; 7:37–40

Why is it hard for Israel to accept that Jesus is *the* Prophet and greater than Moses?

If Jesus is that great, why is it foolish to ignore him?

How do we make Jesus our Lord and King? What does that mean?

WEEK 14: READING 3

Leader Notes

Jesus speaks of the Law, the Prophets, and the Psalms (Luke 24:44). The Prophets he speaks of begins with Joshua through Kings, followed by the prophetic books. Deuteronomy 34 and Joshua 1 are the hinge between the Law and the Prophets. While Israel (starting with Joshua—see Joshua 1:1–9) is waiting for the prophet like Moses, they are to meditate on the Law, day and night, and they will be successful. These words will appear again at the next great hinge between eras in Psalm 1. That is the hinge between the eras of the Prophets and the Writings.

The Law of Moses is pointed toward the Messiah, the coming King. The inability to obey the law is a reminder of how deep the need is, but God has not forgotten Israel. When Jesus comes on the scene it is very hard for Israel to imagine that this carpenter from Nazareth is in the same league with the great Moses.

WEEK 15

Reading 1

BIBLE STORY

Joshua, the new leader, is to be strong and courageous. He is to meditate on the book of the Law day and night. This is the formula for success while a person is waiting for the prophet like Moses.

Joshua 1:1–9; 2

Why is it alright that Joshua is different than Moses?

How is Joshua like Moses (Numbers 13)?

How is the result different this time (Joshua 2:1, 24)?

BIBLE CONVERSATION

Centuries later Israel's kings fail, and Israel is sent away to exile in Babylon. They are given the same words for how to succeed while waiting for the prophet like Moses, the coming King of Israel.

Psalm 1

Why is delighting in and meditating on God's word our best guide no matter what times we live in (Psalm 1:2)?

How can we prosper if our time and place in history is hard?

Who should we stay away from so that we can prosper?

WEEK 15: READING 1

Leader Notes

Joshua has every reason to be intimidated by having to lead after Moses. He is not the *prophet like Moses* (Deuteronomy 34:10) and is waiting for that person like everyone else. But Joshua is a military commander, and he will lead the younger generation of Israel into the land. That is the task of his life. We have a task in our lives for which God has set us in place.

We might be called to work and act in the shadow of someone great, our own parents perhaps, but God expects us to be strong, be courageous, and to meditate on his word day and night. We have great advantage over Joshua because Jesus won victories for us that cannot be lost.

Joshua sends spies like Moses, but he only sends two instead of twelve. Last time they should have listened to the two, one of whom was Joshua. The woman Rahab becomes part of the lineage of the Messiah Jesus according to Matthew's genealogy.

WEEK 15

Reading 2

BIBLE STORY

After the spies return from Jericho the Israelites prepare to take the city.

Joshua 5:13–15; 6:12–27

Why is it a big deal that the commander of the Lord's army meets Joshua?

Why might Joshua be very encouraged by that?

Why is the victory at Jericho a good start?

BIBLE CONVERSATION

With most of the day-to-day details set aside, we later see the faith it takes to get the Israelites into the land.

Hebrews 4:8–11; 11:23–31

Why is Moses' and Joshua's faith so important here in the New Testament and to us now?

What important life project do you now need to work on with courage? Learning? Building good character?

How does knowing Jesus give us the courage and strength we need?

WEEK 15: READING 2

Leader Notes

Israel is coming back into the land after almost five centuries in Egypt and the wilderness. Long ago, angels meet Jacob when he comes back to the land. If this place is the garden before the flood, are they the same angels guarding the way to the tree of life? We do not know the answer to that, but coming back to this place is a big deal. The destruction coming onto those people living there is God's judgment for the horrible things (child sacrifice and more) they are doing in that special place. Israel will be subject to that same judgment later for doing those very things.

These stories are the foundation for the gospel message of the New Testament. Hebrews reminds us that all these acts of courage are carried out in faith. Joshua's success comes after Israel's failure to trust God and enter the land in Numbers 14. But Joshua's success is pointing forward to us entering God's rest in Jesus.

WEEK 15

Reading 3

BIBLE STORY

After a successful career leading the Israelites, Joshua reminds them of all that God has done for them.

Joshua 24

We listen to our parents now, but why do we have to decide about following God for ourselves someday?

Are you ready to say, *Yes, I believe this and will do it*?

Imagine living to 110 years like Joshua. What will it be like speaking only to people younger than ourselves?

BIBLE CONVERSATION

Joshua's review of his life is a reminder that we are part of something greater than ourselves.

Hebrews 12:1–2

How is life like a race?

Who is waiting for us when we finish this race we are running?

What will we ask Joshua when we meet him?

WEEK 15: READING 3

Leader Notes

The younger generation that has a heroic generation to follow will live up to their example, right? Not necessarily. Joshua's life coming to an end is important because the following generations do not follow the Lord faithfully.

We read Scripture and apply it for our own time. Then our children must do the same, but we can only teach and encourage. At some point they must decide and own it for themselves—obey because they believe. That is why we do this reading and conversing.

There is a personal aspect; each must decide. There is a community aspect; Joshua and Caleb lead in their generation. They individually decide to do the right thing even though everyone else dies in the desert for their sins.

WEEK 16

Reading 1

BIBLE STORY

After Joshua's retirement and death, the Israelites again begin to test God.

Judges 2:6–23

What great gifts has God given the Israelites?

Why are we better, and better off, when we are grateful for what we have? To whom are we grateful?

Why is doing the right thing seldom the same as looking at what our neighbor has?

BIBLE CONVERSATION

Just as God gives generously to the Israelites in ancient times, he still gives us much more than we deserve or dare to hope.

Ephesians 1:3–14

How much more does God give to everyone in Jesus?

How personally does God know each of us who follow Jesus (Ephesians 1:13–14)?

WEEK 16: READING 1

Leader Notes

The next generation struggles to stay close with God, a pattern throughout history. It is part of our nature. We teach and encourage but eventually everyone decides for themselves. A young man is taken with a woman and incorporates her family practices into their new family together and *vice versa*. That is how idol worship crept into Israel. That is why the laws seem so strict.

The saying that we cannot legislate morality is partly true. We can legislate it, but people ultimately must decide to follow. This is deeply part of humankind's relationship with God. God lets us decide by giving us choices. It is wiser, happier, and better in every way to choose the Lord, but it is our choice.

The Lord gives laws to check our worst behavior on one hand. On the other hand, he gives extravagant gifts to encourage us to stay with him. What we have with him is promised everywhere in the world system but seldom, if ever, delivered. With the Lord we find actual love, comfort, truth, strength, a path forward, and infinitely more.

WEEK 16

Reading 2

BIBLE STORY

Even though the Israelites always get themselves into trouble, God always raises up someone to save them, that is, a savior.

Judges 4

Why does the Lord let them be in this bad situation (Judges 4:3–4)?

How are we exactly like this?

Why is it better not to need rescuing all the time (even though we always need rescuing)?

BIBLE CONVERSATION

God continues to save people who allow themselves to be saved.

Ephesians 2:1–10

How does the Lord rescue us from our slavery like he saved Israel (Ephesians 2:3–5)?

Do we earn God's gift by impressing him with good deeds (Ephesians 2:8–9)?

But, for what reason does he re-create us in Jesus (Ephesians 2:10)?

WEEK 16: READING 2

Leader Notes

We love liberty and autonomy but without living by central truths we are quickly in trouble. Why do we consistently test the Lord's patience? Because we are self-centered and selfish.

Two women are the heroes of this story. The Bible from the beginning regards men and women as fully equal because they are both fully made in the image of God. Their roles are often different, which comes into the discussion here with Deborah chiding Barak about getting credit for the battle. The strength of women here is shown in getting men to use their kind of strength and together winning the day.

Israel is a tribe-nation. Their individual fates are all tied together. We have much more individuality and personal connection to God in Jesus. Our individual autonomy is much greater because of Messiah Jesus. But our culture has taken individual autonomy to extremes. We now struggle to remember how important it is for Jesus followers to stay together.

WEEK 16

Reading 3

BIBLE STORY

During the turbulent time after Joshua's death God raises up some of Israel's most famous national heroes.

Judges 6:33—7:23

Why is the Lord so patient with our fears?

What do you hope the Lord will not ask you to do? (Does he know you don't want him to ask?)

Who fills in the gap between our fears and getting the job done?

BIBLE CONVERSATION

Later heroes form the foundation of God's new living house.

Ephesians 2:11–22

From whom did the Bible and our faith come (Ephesians 2:11-12)?

If Jesus, the apostles, and prophets were all Jewish (Ephesians 2:20), how great is it that everyone now gets to be part of this house God is building?

What is the difference between going to church and being the church?

WEEK 16: READING 3

Leader Notes

The judges are all weak and flawed people who bring their everyday paganism into their work. They are supposed to be living by the Law of Moses, but they seldom do. God is patient but something more is needed. Doing the right thing in a difficult time can be complicated and does not always resolve things to a clear solution.

God's persistence in keeping his promise to Abraham eventually brings reconciliation to the world through Jesus the Jewish Messiah. It is a spiritual truth that is simple and singular, in contrast to the murky time of the judges.

WEEK 17

Reading 1

BIBLE STORY

In the time of the judges, God raises up more leaders for the Israelites after Gideon, some better than others.

Judges 13

Does God mean for good things to happen in Samson's life?

Does Samson do everything said of him when he grows up?

Are we doing everything God has intended for us?

BIBLE CONVERSATION

Just as God invests in Samson's life, he makes great riches available to us.

Ephesians 3:14–21

What good things does God intend for us?

Do we have a choice whether to be part of those good things?

What blessing might others get from our life if we listen to God?

WEEK 17: READING 1

Leader Notes

Samson had a blessed beginning, a lot to live for. This story is parallel to Hannah and the birth of Israel's last judge, Samuel. In the Bible story, God sometimes uses being childless to accentuate a special person.

Our blessings in the Messiah are not always as obvious as Samson's strength, but they are ultimately much bigger, stronger, and more real. Samson's strength goes away; it is temporary. God's gifts in the Messiah Jesus last forever and span the universe.

Even so, we have the choice whether to access God's gifts. Samson takes the parts he likes and ignores most of the commitment that goes with the gift. He does not fool God. If we want the deep understanding, love, and strength that comes with the Lord's gifts we have to be all in. He will not be fooled if we use his salvation as an insurance policy and no more.

WEEK 17

Reading 2

BIBLE STORY

After Samson's auspicious birth he becomes a promising leader.

Judges 15:9–20

Why doesn't God have Samson completely overthrow the Philistines?

Do we have to be perfect for God to use us?

What might God do in our life that is uniquely ours? (Who else ever used a jawbone?)

BIBLE CONVERSATION

Samson does great deeds, and God calls us now to even greater things.

Ephesians 4:1–16

What gift might God give to us besides physical strength (Ephesians 4:7–8, 11–13)?

The purpose of the gifts is to make us strong together; can we work with other different people?

Why is it strong to love someone that is hard to love?

WEEK 17: READING 2

Leader Notes

Samson is an imperfect leader. God uses him anyway. That is a big truth for us. When we fail, we find out that it is God working and we worry about our failure more than he does.

Samson's strength is a local and limited glory. God gifts us in Jesus to work together changing lives, family systems, and the world.

WEEK 17

Reading 3

BIBLE STORY

Samson's great deeds for God are overshadowed by his ungodly behavior.

Judges 16:4–31

Why is it good to have our parents help us with some decisions, like whom to marry?

How does God love us but also let us live with the consequences of our own foolishness?

Why does God want us to keep walking with him, especially when we fail?

BIBLE CONVERSATION

Like Samson, God asks us to engage in battle on his behalf.

Ephesians 6:10–20

How big is the spiritual war we are in?

Do we possess all the armor of God listed here?

How does our fight look different than Samson's?

WEEK 17: READING 3

Leader Notes

Samson would be barely identifiable as an Israelite by his behavior. But God chose him, worked with him, and worked through him. The success of Israel's leaders and their favor with God is revealed in part by how well they hold back the Philistines. This is preparing us readers for Israel's need for a king.

Our failures are the main reason we quit. It is important that we press on with God, through our failures. God can work amid our failures. That is when we really learn and grow.

Paul's armor of God passage in Ephesians is taken from Isaiah 59:15b–17, where God himself is a warrior fighting on behalf of his people. We, the living presence of the Lord, do that mission now. The Lord chooses to dwell in his people and so bring light and goodness into the world with our godly lives.

WEEK 18

Reading 1

BIBLE STORY

In the dark time of the judges, when everyone does what is right in his own eyes, God continues to work in the family of Judah.

Ruth 1

How does Ruth's faithfulness create a pathway for God's goodness?

If our life is emptied out, why is our story not yet over?

What are some ways we go back home, like Naomi, when we are in trouble?

BIBLE CONVERSATION

Truth finds its way down through the generations through faithful families.

Deuteronomy 6:4–9

Why is it often harder to be faithful when times are easy?

How can we be a help for those seeking God?

How can God's word be in every part of our lives?

WEEK 18: READING 1

Leader Notes

Naomi has status back in Bethlehem, but her life is emptied out; no husband or sons. Ruth has no status, but she stands up and commits herself to the God of Israel and to Naomi. There seems to be no future for her, but God is always seeking one heart that will say "Yes, Lord."

Famine and death bring out Ruth's commitment. We dread difficulty and hard times, but we seem to lose our focus during good times. We are in much more spiritual danger when things are going well. That is why Jesus tells us how hard it is for a wealthy person to enter the kingdom of heaven.

So we practice spiritual disciplines. We teach our children the word of God, and in the process remind ourselves, and learn as well. That is the point of being in this reader with your child!

WEEK 18

Reading 2

BIBLE STORY

Ruth commits herself to Naomi and to the Lord. In her deepest loss, the Lord begins to open doors for her.

Ruth 2

Why does Ruth go out and work in the fields during harvest?

Why does Ruth "accidently" choose Boaz's field to work in?

What kind of filling up is happening to Ruth and Naomi?

BIBLE CONVERSATION

Ruth's great-grandson David will be a great king in Zion. David knows that from his body will come an even greater king beyond himself.

Psalm 2

David is a shepherd. How does God bring great things from simple people committed to him?

Do you believe that God can bring good, even great good, from your life with him?

Will you walk with God even if, like Ruth, you never see the greatest glory from your life until heaven?

WEEK 18: READING 2

Leader Notes

Both of these *texts* are placed in the Bible later in the era of the Writings (exile and post-exile), looking back. But the *events* of Ruth's faithfulness and David's ascent to Zion as king come earlier, in the time of the judges, kings, and prophets. The Scripture gives us pictures of coming glory that flow out of our everyday lives (like Ruth, and later David, working in the fields.) We do not know what glory will come from our everyday work. But it can be chock full of God's eternal values working in us: love, joy, grace, truth, and more.

The greater glory of Psalm 2 is in heaven, where Jesus reigns as king and in the days ahead when he takes the throne in Zion. We are part of heaven now and future glories later. Our willingness to go out into the fields of our life and work with integrity brings us into God's story and his glory.

WEEK 18

Reading 3

BIBLE STORY

Ruth's hard work in Boaz's fields allows God to open an opportunity for her.

Ruth 3

How does being a "woman of noble character" (Ruth 3:11) create ways for God to make Ruth a hero in the Bible story?

How is Ruth both humble and bold?

How can we be a person of noble character in our current situation?

BIBLE CONVERSATION

Ruth's noble character becomes a model for all godly women.

Proverbs 31:10–31

How much courage does it take to do the right thing when we don't know how things will turn out?

Why is Ruth's example so intimidating to wives, moms, and everyone?

How might we be a blessing to our family, friends, and acquaintances today?

WEEK 18: READING 3

Leader Notes

In the Jesus order of the ancient Hebrew Bible (Luke 24:44), the book of Proverbs is often placed next to the book of Ruth because of the connection of that phrase, "woman of noble character." The Proverbs, ascribed to King Solomon, has one of Ruth's grandsons, who is king, telling his own son to find a wife like Ruth.

Ruth becomes a standout in Israel's history as an example of character overcoming the barrier of being a foreigner. She is in Matthew's genealogy of Jesus the Messiah.

Her willingness to act on her opportunity is key. She does everything that is in her power but does not force her situation. She boldly asks the question, but then waits for an answer, allowing God to work through the other characters in her story. She exercises strength and influence in a particularly feminine way.

WEEK 19

Reading 1

BIBLE STORY

Ruth waits to see what her hero Boaz can do. He is a skillful man.

Ruth 4

How long does Ruth work after making her commitment to Naomi?

How does God fill up the lives of Ruth and Naomi after they are emptied?

How can we commit ourselves to the Lord?

BIBLE CONVERSATION

Ruth passes on character and faith to her great-grandson David. When we press forward with the Lord, he shows us more and more great things.

Psalm 16

What do we have in our life that is good?

What can we be doing with that?

How might the greatness of God turn out to be different than what we now imagine?

WEEK 19: READING 1

Leader Notes

From after the fact, we see Ruth's greatness, but she acts faithfully not knowing how it will turn out. She does not know the end or the genealogy of the book of Ruth.

David himself will be in the same situation, just a shepherd boy, youngest of eight sons. Just being committed to something is not enough. We commit to something worthy of our commitment: the Lord and the character that he develops in us.

Many of us struggle to find greatness within ourselves. That is why Ruth and David's descendant Jesus came. He was the one who changed everything so that the lowest of us could become great in the kingdom of God.

WEEK 19

Reading 2

BIBLE STORY

At the end of the time of the judges, God brings more light to his people through another family that trusts him.

1 Samuel 1

Why is having a baby such a big deal?

Why was Hannah taking this problem in her life to God?

How long should we keep praying about things that are bothering us (1 Samuel 1:7)?

BIBLE CONVERSATION

God often begins with a baby so that no one can say, "It was my strength."

Psalm 8

What does it mean that Jesus came to us as a baby?

How are babies important while they are still babies?

Why does God make us so important? Are we really that good?

Leader Notes

The birth of Samuel marks him as special in the dark time of the judges. He is the last judge of Israel and a prophet as well.

Babies are one of God's most effective training methods. Having a baby forces most parents to make someone else (the baby) the center of their world, often for the first time in their life. Babies are the weakest, most vulnerable, but most precious of creatures. The birth of Jesus the Messiah will be the apex of the Bible's birth stories.

Psalm 8 brings out the conundrum of being human. In Genesis 1–3 we are demonstrably foolish but also still made in the image of God and in charge of the creation. How to bring our greatness and our weakness into the same space is always difficult; it is why we need to be always connected to the Lord.

WEEK 19

Reading 3

BIBLE STORY

After Samuel is born, he is sent as a young boy to serve in the tabernacle in a time of evil.

1 Samuel 2:12–26

If we treat the things of God with disrespect, do we really believe him?

Why does serving the Lord make our standards for living higher?

When people with authority (Eli's sons) do bad things, why is it harder for everyone else to keep doing the right things?

BIBLE CONVERSATION

Eli's sons are evil hypocrites. God is looking for people who will live rightly.

Psalm 15

What is the list of things that define a blameless person?

How does following Jesus help us do all those things?

Does the last line of the psalm mean we will never have problems if we are good?

WEEK 19: READING 3

Leader Notes

Samuel is being used to turn Israel in a new direction, even though he won't like it. Samuel has no political infrastructure supporting him. He simply serves the Lord with his whole heart.

Eli's sons remind us of Aaron's sons who were killed by the Lord in Leviticus 10. The Lord is patient to a point. He gives us time to grow, learn, and change. But Eli's sons never change. This is a weakness of the hereditary priesthood, father-to-son. Some take advantage of the privilege without owning the responsibility. This will plague Samuel and the kings as well.

David's psalm addresses the sacred tent (the tabernacle) and being close to God. There are many joys in our life with God, but there are responsibilities as well. This principle is still huge in following Jesus. God does not tolerate entitlement. We cannot say, as some do, "I am going to do this bad thing. God will have to forgive me because I am saved by grace."

WEEK 20

Reading 1

BIBLE STORY

When the Lord has had enough of Eli's evil sons, he begins to work through the young boy Samuel.

1 Samuel 3

Why is God holding Eli responsible for his grown children's behavior?

How might the Lord do something new in the world with your life?

How do we most often hear the voice of the Lord?

BIBLE CONVERSATION

We discern what is true with God's wisdom but leave the judgment up to the Lord.

Matthew 7:1–6

Who would you allow to take a speck of something out of your eye?

Who would you not allow that close to you?

Who does the Lord have in our lives to help us make that decision?

WEEK 20: READING 1

Leader Notes

Eli's sons are corrupt, like Aaron's sons. Aaron is suspect because he made the golden calf, but Eli seems like a good fellow. The difference is that Aaron apparently does not know about his sons' foolishness, and they make a single, fatal mistake (Leviticus 10). Eli hears about his sons' ongoing blasphemous behavior in this holy place and, though he warns them, he does not make them stop. It happens on his watch. Sometimes being nice is not enough; action is required.

The Lord starts with Samuel as a boy. That's important. Our culture has it that we have some destiny to spend our youth without responsibility because we will have to grow up soon enough. That is not how God operates.

Hearing the voice of the Lord for us begins with our spiritual disciplines in the word, in prayer, by the Spirit. When we let those things shape our hearts and minds, we begin to hear what it is the Lord has to say.

Jesus teaches us how to judge. We let people we trust into our heart conversations. We take things out of each other's eyes. But some people we steer clear of. There are some people we do not trust to take something out of our eye. Those kinds of decisions are the wisdom God teaches us.

WEEK 20

Reading 2

BIBLE STORY

After the boy Samuel prophesies against Eli and his sons, God's judgment comes to pass.

1 Samuel 4

Why is Israel treating the ark of God like it is a magic wand they can use?

With the ark gone, why are things bad but not hopeless? Where is the hope in this story?

Why do so many forgettable days go by and then everything happens at once? Where is God in all of it?

BIBLE CONVERSATION

Everyone has excuses for their sins, but God's plain truth is everywhere.

Psalm 19

What is the message of God being spoken in all the creation around us?

What is the message in the written-down word of God?

Why should we be joyful and thankful to the Lord?

WEEK 20: READING 2

Leader Notes

To whom much is given, much is required, says Jesus. Israel has the Law and the ark, and yet they live in shadow, superstition, and weakness all the time of the judges. So, God brings overdue judgment all on one day, as he sometimes does. Samuel is ready to lead. He is the last of the judges of Israel, though he does not yet know that. The ark is gone, but God is not; what will happen?

The ark is gone, but the promise remains. David will remind Israel in his psalm that the truth about God is everywhere in creation and in the Scripture. Psalm 19 is a great piece on many levels. The word-picture of creation pouring forth speech has become intensely focused in our lifetimes with the new knowledge that vast amounts of information are stored in every cell of every living thing.

WEEK 20

Reading 3

BIBLE STORY

After the ark is captured, the Philistines learn what the Israelites already know: that the Lord is far more than a local god. They cannot control God by having the ark.

1 Samuel 5

Why is the trouble for the Philistines from more than just the ark itself?

Why is it so like God to get the Philistines to decide to send the ark, their prize, back home to Israel?

How is this like Pharaoh sending Israel out of Egypt?

Why is our relationship with God ultimately more important than the religious forms we keep?

BIBLE CONVERSATION

The Philistines bring unexpected trouble on themselves. David tells of the coming Messiah who will take our troubles on himself.

Psalm 22

How is this a picture of Jesus' death and resurrection one thousand years before it happened?

Why is life so intense and out of our control sometimes?

Does God stop bad things from happening, or give us strength to get through them, or both, or what?

WEEK 20: READING 3

Leader Notes

The Israelites treat the ark with almost as much superstition as the Philistines do. They bring it into battle like an amulet, a good luck charm. God is merciful to the ignorant Philistines by not breaking out and destroying them completely. They don't know the Lord. His response is measured, and they get the message: *This thing belongs to someone else.*

David will struggle with the ark later, but he writes of the suffering that a coming king, his great descendant, will endure for the sake of his people.

WEEK 21

Reading 1

BIBLE STORY

After the ark returns to Israel, Samuel judges Israel for many years. Ironically, his sons are corrupt like Eli's sons.

1 Samuel 8

Why are Samuel and the Lord displeased that the people want a king (1 Samuel 8:6–7)?

Why does the Lord say to let the people have a king?

Why does God let us choose things that may make our own lives more difficult?

BIBLE CONVERSATION

The Israelites want a king like the other nations, but they need a king who loves and trusts the Lord.

Psalm 23

What happens to domestic sheep that no one is looking after?

Why do we need our parents to look after us when we are young?

Why do we need the Lord to look after us all the days of our lives?

WEEK 21: READING 1

Leader Notes

Moving from judges to kings is a complicated but important change that Israel makes. It seems like the Lord is against them having a king but has already prophesied a coming king. The Lord will choose the first two kings. Saul apparently is the embodiment of what Israel asks for; a king like other nations have. He looks like what the people are asking for, and God gives him everything he needs for encouragement and success.

It is important to see that these are not simple moral fables, but rather interwoven stories of God bringing his people to the Messiah. Their lives are complicated, like ours. Things don't always have a clear, immediately apparent meaning. Everyone must make decisions without knowing what will happen next.

David's now-famous Twenty-third Psalm reflects his understanding of the Lord's care and protection in a word-picture he as a shepherd understands. He does not spend all his shepherding time thinking about being somewhere else. But rather he throws himself into it and is good at it. That will eventually make him a great shepherd of all Israel as their king.

WEEK 21

Reading 2

BIBLE STORY

The Israelites want to have a king like the other nations, so God gives them one.

1 Samuel 9:1–6, 14–21; 10:1–7

Will Saul, being tall and handsome, make people think he is the king they wanted?

Why is a great historical event, Israel having their first king, all tied up with something as boring as Saul looking for his dad's lost donkeys?

If the Spirit of the Lord comes on us powerfully (1 Samuel 10:6), won't we think God is for us?

BIBLE CONVERSATION

There are many glorious kings in this world, but who is the King of Glory?

Psalm 24

Why is it hard for kings to be good people?

Why do we not trust kings?

Who is the only king we should absolutely trust? Why?

WEEK 21: READING 2

Leader Notes

Saul is given everything a King of Israel needs, anointing from man and from God. He is anointed king by the last judge of Israel, Samuel, who is a great prophet. He is affirmed by the school of prophets introduced here. This group stays in the background but is largely responsible for the shape of the Hebrew Bible as we have it. They are God's great influencers in the time of the kings of Israel and beyond. Saul is affirmed in every way and given what he needs to be king.

So, if the Lord is not pleased with Israel wanting a king, he does not program it for failure to prove his point. If they would have a king, then this king will be given everything he needs.

David in the psalm later reminds us of who the real king is. The Lord is where all of our good and high ideals of being king emerge. We struggle with the idea of what a king is. Our entire political structure and history in America is as anti-king as possible because kings can be bad. But God is king. Messiah means anointed one, or king. So, King Saul was called "messiah"; the anointed one of God. Every king was called that. "Christ" is the Greek word for "messiah." "Jesus Christ" means the same as "Jesus the Messiah." That means "Jesus the King." So, every time we read or say "Jesus Christ," we are saying "Jesus the King." That is who he is in the Bible's language.

WEEK 21

Reading 3

BIBLE STORY

Saul is the first king in Israel, and he fails to trust God.

1 Samuel 13:1–14

If Saul is king forty-two years, does he have time to figure things out?

What is the difference between offering a sacrifice and asking the Lord?

Is it more important to pass a class in school, or learn the subject, or both? Why?

BIBLE CONVERSATION

Saul never understands what David does; the Lord is good, he loves us, and we can trust him. Jesus, Son of David, explains this to us again.

Matthew 7:7–12

Jesus says our Father in heaven loves us; is it true?

Does this mean that we get everything we want and nothing bad will happen to us?

What does it mean?

Leader Notes

Saul has a long career as king with every privilege and advantage. His lack of relationship with the Lord shows up in his poor decisions; he does not understand God or want to. There is a string of his foolish mistakes in these stories. He is set in contrast to David, who is coming after him.

To fear the Lord is the beginning of wisdom. Saul is afraid of the Lord, and that is different than respecting and being in awe. He sees rituals as a way to placate God, that is, keep him away by giving him what he seems to want.

Jesus assures us that we are at the center of God's attention. That should give us a new attitude and open the way to deeper understanding.

WEEK 22

Reading 1

BIBLE STORY

After the Lord rejects Saul as king, he sends Samuel to anoint the next king.

1 Samuel 16:1–13

How dangerous is it for David to be anointed king while Saul is king? Why?

Why does David look like an unlikely choice (1 Samuel 16:6–7, 11)?

What does it mean that the Lord notices us, even though we may not feel very noticeable?

BIBLE CONVERSATION

Jesus looks at the inside of everyone. We will not fool him even if we fool ourselves and everyone around us.

Matthew 7:15–23

Why is it a good idea (why is it wise) to dress well and look presentable?

What is the connection between looking sharp and being sharp?

Why is our heart the only thing that ultimately matters?

WEEK 22: READING 1

Leader Notes

To anoint a king while there is a sitting king is extremely dangerous. If Saul finds out, he will kill all of David's family without thinking twice. He will kill Samuel even though he might think twice about that. Young David and his family must keep this secret. It forces them to be clever in order to survive.

David, as the youngest of eight boys, is tending sheep, that is, tending the family fortune. The sheep herd is the family savings account. It is tough, unattractive work. He protects the sheep from hungry and greedy predators. He apparently is good at his work. He doesn't save himself for a fantasy destiny (*Maybe someday I'll be great*). He learns how to care for the sheep and puts himself at risk in mortal combat with whoever or whatever comes after those in his care.

David learns to pray and meditate in those long hours. He is more than he appears to the world around, the youngest of eight stuck out herding the sheep. His oldest brothers seek the glory of soldiering in Saul's army, but do not have the heart for which the Lord is looking.

Jesus, an uneducated craftsman born in poverty, seems like no one to the world, and he picks regular people for disciples. He teaches this principle: that God looks at the heart. He knows the wisdom of doing the best with what we have. We are not called to be lazy or slovenly in our appearance but to be fully who we are, knowing that God will change the world with us.

WEEK 22

Reading 2

BIBLE STORY

After David is secretly anointed king, he begins to help Saul.

1 Samuel 17:1–16, 32–54

What is David's blend of wisdom and faith (1 Samuel 17:36–37)?

What does David's heart clearly understand that shows he is the right pick to be king (1 Samuel 17:45–47)?

What job do you have now that God is using to build your character and skills (even if you don't like it)?

BIBLE CONVERSATION

Saul finally sees the kind of king God is looking for because David is right in front of him.

Psalm 40:1–8

Eventually even David sees a better king than himself coming (Psalm 40:7); who is that?

Do we have to wait until we are grown up to serve the Lord or until he notices us?

What different kinds of things might God have for us to do now and later?

WEEK 22: READING 2

Leader Notes

David and Goliath is not just a morality story about facing down the giants in our lives. It is about knowing who the Lord is and living to it. It is about operating from our heart rather than being limited by our status and looks.

Saul is afraid and hanging back, which is why his soldiers are doing the same. They have all the right gear, and they look great, but their hearts are not in this. Saul putting his armor on David is the perfect picture. David can only do this task with what he knows right now, a sling and stone. He will soon wear armor and carry a sword. We all have things we must do now before we are ready for something that will only come later.

Psalm 40 is a messianic psalm, intersecting with Isaiah 53 and Hebrews 10. We always have our great King, Jesus, out in front as example of the heart that God seeks.

WEEK 22

Reading 3

BIBLE STORY

After slaying Goliath, David works for Saul full-time.

1 Samuel 18:1–16

Why is Saul afraid of David (1 Samuel 18:12)? Who is really in danger?

How important is it that the Spirit of the Lord is on David and has abandoned Saul?

How important is it that God now promises to never leave those who follow Jesus (Romans 8:38–39)?

BIBLE CONVERSATION

As Saul goes further from the Lord, David draws closer.

Psalm 42

Why is our instinct to run away from God?

Why should we run toward God when we are in trouble, especially when we do wrong?

WEEK 22: READING 3

Leader Notes

Saul is older now and David is a threat. Saul expects his son Jonathan to be king, but he is told by Samuel that that will not happen. This is about survival. Any new king from another family will kill Saul's whole family; his children and grandchildren. That is the world they live in.

David sees with clarity; Saul is unsure. The Lord's presence with David and not Saul reinforces that. There is deep irony here. Saul seeks comfort from David, in whom the Lord now dwells, but David is his biggest rival and threat. Still, ironically, David is working for Saul and doing great things for him, and that drives Saul's jealousy into madness.

There is no manipulation or cleverness that replaces a relationship with God. The psalm expresses the relationship we need to seek, because that is what God is seeking with us.

WEEK 23

Reading 1

BIBLE STORY

Saul's jealousy grows worse, and David flees for his life, but the Lord is with David.

1 Samuel 26

Despite Saul's kind words, why is David wise to not trust him?

Why does the Lord let this situation go on and not just fix it?

What difficult things are you praying about in your life?

BIBLE CONVERSATION

David writes this psalm while hiding from Saul. He learns a deeper trust in the Lord as Saul tries again and again to kill him.

Psalm 57

List some things in life for which we do not know what will happen.

What good can never happen if we do not struggle in this life?

If the Lord is with us in ongoing difficulties, what does that mean about our relationship with him?

WEEK 23: READING 1

Leader Notes

Saul is never going to stop pursuing David. David represents a threat to the actual survival of Saul's dynasty and his family. Saul is conflicted but driven. This goes on for ten years. In that time David builds his family, his trusted inner army, and his vision for Israel. In that time the Lord develops David's wisdom, faith, and strength of character. He develops a king for Israel.

There are things inside us that never grow if we get everything we want when we want it. The Lord forces us to grow up with difficult life situations. Our life balance is that we must live in the joy and peace that the Lord brings while we are struggling and growing. The danger of success is that if we stop struggling, we stop growing.

Our relationship with the Lord changes as we grow, just like our relationship with our parents changes over time. We start to understand who he really is by what he lets us go through and by how he saves us.

WEEK 23

Reading 2

BIBLE STORY

Saul is afraid of the Lord and of David. He needs them both to help him, but it is too late.

1 Samuel 28:3–25; 31

Even though the Lord brings it about, how does Saul create this sad ending to his own life?

How do our bad choices create no-win situations for us?

Why is it good for us to learn to trust the Lord when we are young?

BIBLE CONVERSATION

Saul, sadly, is a religious man who does not trust God. Jesus teaches about this common state of being.

Matthew 7:24–29

Who or what does the rock represent in Jesus' teaching?

What is the sand?

How do we build our house on the rock? By only going to church services?

Leader Notes

Saul is an old man who looks successful; three warrior sons, king for forty-two years. He spends his life stubbornly refusing to center his heart with the Lord. He tries to placate God with religious rites but is afraid to be close with him. It is not a private, sideline issue. As the king of Israel, he is leading the Lord's chosen people. They need to know that their king is in close relationship to the Lord.

Saul, for many years, tries to grasp what he cannot, an assured future. He refuses to hang onto the Lord. He refuses to say, "Whatever you have for me, Lord, here am I."

Jesus' teaching about the house built on the sand exactly captures Saul's life. Everything crashes because Saul refuses to be where the Lord is. God gives him plenty of time, a whole life, to work it out. What David learns as a shepherd boy, Saul never gets, even in the very presence of the Spirit of the Lord.

It is harder to change as we get older. If we begin walking with the Lord while we are young, we will more readily let him change us, especially if we have parents in whom we trust.

WEEK 23

Reading 3

BIBLE STORY

When Saul and Jonathan die on Mt. Gilboa, Israel loses its first king, and David loses his best friend.

2 Samuel 1:17–27

Why does David honor Saul's life by lamenting about what was good in it?

Why is life so complicated that David's best friend dies with his father who is trying to destroy David?

What can we learn in the middle of a mess?

BIBLE CONVERSATION

The sadness of the king's death is overshadowed by the sadness of what he could have had.

Psalm 91

Does this psalm mean that nothing bad can ever happen to us? Why?

How do we live in the Lord's protection?

What is the Lord's protection for those who live in his shelter?

WEEK 23: READING 3

Leader Notes

David always honors the fact that Saul is the Lord's anointed, the messiah, the king. That honor is an insight into David's trust in the Lord. However disappointing Saul is, the truth about him, that he is the Lord's anointed, stands. David trusts that Saul will be the anointed one until God changes the situation.

David and Jonathan are bound as lifelong friends. Their bond as warriors is forged from life-and-death situations together on the battlefield. David's lament is a deep sadness that things did not have to be this way. The psalm reflects the faith required to enter the field of battle knowing that our life and fate is in the hands of the Almighty. We will not die one day sooner than our day.

It is a mistake to take the psalm as a promise from God for a comfortable, safe situation. It simply allows us not to be desperate and afraid like Saul. Our comfort and safety are that our heart and soul are God's all the way through and beyond this life.

In Matthew 4:5–7 the devil uses Psalm 91 to tempt Jesus to jump off the temple. The Psalm seems to say nothing bad can happen to you. Jesus rebukes this interpretation as a form of testing God.

WEEK 24

Reading 1

BIBLE STORY

After Saul's death, David is established as king and God makes a great promise to him.

2 Samuel 5:1–13; 7:1–18

Why, at thirty years old, is David better prepared to be king than when he killed Goliath as a teenager?

What amazing promise does the Lord make to King David (2 Samuel 7:12–16)?

What great promises do we receive as followers of King Jesus, the Son of David?

BIBLE CONVERSATION

God has great plans for all his children.

Psalm 103:1–14

How does Jesus bring about taking away our sins (Psalm 103:10–12)?

Why does God help us (Psalm 103:13–14)?

How can we live as the Lord's children?

WEEK 24: READING 1

Leader Notes

It takes David seven years as king to unite all twelve tribes. He conquers Jerusalem and makes it the center of Israel with his palace and the tabernacle (which is later the temple.)

From the books of the Law, we know that the great coming king will be a son of Abraham from the tribe of Judah, and a prophet like Moses. Now in this vision of Nathan the prophet we get another crucial piece of information. We find out that this king will come from David's family. This is bringing the coming Messiah into sharper focus.

From this psalm we get a picture of the relationship between God and his people. Jesus Messiah will bring about, in a much clearer way, this forgiveness of sins and healing. He will redeem our lives from the pit in a way that David is only beginning to understand.

WEEK 24

Reading 2

BIBLE STORY

As king, David takes a woman and kills her husband. After he commits murder and adultery, he goes on as if nothing had happened, like other kings do.

2 Samuel 12:1–24

Why is the King of Israel not allowed to get away with what other kings commonly do?

How is success more dangerous than struggle and failure (2 Samuel 12:7–10)?

How can wealth make us ungrateful and foolish?

BIBLE CONVERSATION

David responds rightly to the word of the Lord concerning his sin.

Psalm 51:1–17

What had David seen in his youth that made him terrified of the Holy Spirit leaving him (Psalm 51:11)?

Why in Israel does the king have to live *under* the law and not *be* the law? What is the difference?

Why does David know that God does not want a religious rite to make this better (Psalm 51:16–17)?

WEEK 24: READING 2

Leader Notes

Nathan's reproach would have been very dangerous before any other king in the world, potentially with David as well. Kings always make themselves the law rather than obeying it. It is part of our nature.

This happens after David is well established. His battle commanders are encouraging him to stay home because he is so famous and successful that he is a liability on the battlefield. All the enemy must do is kill David and it is all over.

Jesus says that it is hard for a wealthy person to enter the kingdom of heaven. David and Bathsheba are a perfect example of why that is so: power corrupts. When we succeed, we suddenly think we did it; we forget God.

The psalm, written in the midst of this trouble, lets us into the heart of David. This is where he is so different than Saul.

WEEK 24

Reading 3

BIBLE STORY

After David sins with Bathsheba, he has many troubles with his family, but he rules Israel until his old age. His son Solomon takes the throne after him.

1 Kings 2:1–12; 3:1–15

After all of David's troubles and successes what is his main advice to Solomon (1 Kings 2:2–4)?

David's mistake, Bathsheba, is Solomon's mother and an ancestor of Jesus (Matthew 1:6); what does that tell us about God's love?

Why is the Lord pleased that Solomon wants wisdom?

BIBLE CONVERSATION

David writes down many prayers called psalms, and his son Solomon writes down many wise sayings called proverbs.

Proverbs 1:1–7

Why do we need understanding and knowledge from the Lord since we have the internet?

What are prudence and discretion? Why are they important?

What kind of people hate wisdom and learning (Proverbs 1:7)?

WEEK 24: READING 3

Leader Notes

The transition of power between David and Solomon is a near disaster, but David is strong even on his deathbed. David is still tangled in the politics that he hands off to Solomon. He helps Solomon survive, but he tells him to stay with the Lord and the Law of Moses.

The psalms give us insights into David's heart that are not in the stories about him. The Psalms become the heart of Israel's worship and prayer life. Solomon's tradition of wisdom in Proverbs becomes the foundation of Israel's wisdom by which to raise children. Prayer, worship, study, and wisdom create a foundation for the lasting generation-to-generation presence of the Lord in young lives.

WEEK 25

Reading 1

BIBLE STORY

Wise King Solomon fulfills his father David's dream of building a temple for the Lord.

1 Kings 5:13—6:13

How does Solomon honor his father David while being a completely different kind of person?

As a replacement for the mobile tent of worship (the tabernacle), how is the solid temple different in meaning?

BIBLE CONVERSATION

King Solomon shows his sons where wisdom comes from.

Proverbs 3:1–12

Is there ever a situation where this is not true?

If we trust the Lord with all our hearts, will that change the life-situation we are in? How?

What does it mean to honor the Lord with our wealth?

WEEK 25: READING 1

Leader Notes

Building the temple solidifies David's dream about a central place for the twelve tribes to unite in worship. The tent (tabernacle) in which God chooses to dwell is replaced by a temple that does not move. God needs no house in which to live, but we need a place to meet him. The temple establishes the nation of Israel in the land and in Jerusalem.

The place to meet God, give thanks, and deal with uncleanness and sin is not going anywhere. It is home. God is staying here in the midst of the people he created from Abraham, Isaac, and Jacob. The human weakness in this arrangement imagines that God is only in the temple.

This temple project is huge in every way. It gives Israel status in the world as a nation. Staying with the Lord through all this magnificence is critical. Solomon is solidifying the tribe of Judah's leadership position in the nation. The rest of the nation notices. The temple enterprise increases the status of the priests and the sacrificial system. Will all this go to anyone's head? Of course! Success is far more dangerous to the human soul than struggle.

One of the most real ways to keep track of where our heart is with God is by giving part of our wealth back to the Lord. Few of us think of ourselves as wealthy, but even fewer ever miss a meal. God knows how our hearts operate. To give does not necessarily mean that we trust the Lord. But if we do not give it is a strong sign that we do not trust in the Lord, despite whatever we say.

WEEK 25

Reading 2

BIBLE STORY

When Solomon completes the temple, he dedicates it to the Lord.

1 Kings 8:1–21; 9:1–9

Why is it impossible for us to be in the presence of the Lord unless he allows (1 Kings 8:1–11)?

Why is the warning important (1 Kings 9:6–9)?

How is this temple like the garden of Eden?

BIBLE CONVERSATION

Jesus teaches us that the temple is wherever God chooses to live.

John 2:19–22; 1 Corinthians 3:16–17; 6:19–20

How is Jesus the temple, the place we meet God while he walks on earth?

How are we the temple, the place others meet God while we walk on earth?

If God lives in us, how big a deal is that, and how should it affect the way we live?

WEEK 25: READING 2

Leader Notes

The garden of Eden is a temple where Adam and Eve live in the presence of the Lord. We spend our lives trying to recreate that place with all our gardens and safe, restful places. Solomon's temple is full of peaceful nature images. Sin makes the concept of the temple starker; we really need to be in the Lord's presence, but it is harder now than in Eden. It is harder because we bring our uncleanness, our stench of death, into the presence of the living God, the source of all life.

Jesus is the living presence of God on earth while he walks on earth. People are terrified of the uncleanness of disease and death. Jesus is not afraid of being made unclean. He brings cleanness, wholeness, and life back into our world.

The biggest shock of all is that God chooses us, followers of Jesus, to be his living presence walking on this earth. This happens by the Holy Spirit indwelling all who believe, that is live for, the Lord Jesus. It is a huge responsibility that we are the place where people see God in this life, but that is God's choice.

WEEK 25

Reading 3

BIBLE STORY

After completing the temple and royal palace, Solomon expands his interests beyond what is pleasing to the Lord.

1 Kings 10:1–13; 11:1–13

Is the Lord unhappy because Solomon is breaking the rules, or damaging himself and others, or both?

Why is being able to do anything we feel like so tempting and so dangerous to our souls?

If Solomon is wise, why doesn't he live wisely?

BIBLE CONVERSATION

Solomon warns his sons about some of the people that have ensnared him.

Proverbs 5:1–14

The woman described here is different than the woman called Wisdom; how is she different?

What is great about being elementary school-age?

How can this kind of temptation work differently for girls (think of Eve and the snake)?

WEEK 25: READING 3

Leader Notes

The question after David is: When will the promised (2 Samuel 7) Messiah King come? All kings of Israel are messiahs, anointed ones, but when will the One with the eternal kingdom come? Solomon looks like a good candidate: he builds the temple, he is the wisest man, he is the son of David.

It looks like he is the one until he is overtaken by his own desires. He acquires many foreign wives and loves them all. He also worships their gods. He is not the One.

Solomon knows this. He warns his sons about it, but wealth and power (getting whatever we want) are almost irresistible temptations for us sons of Adam and daughters of Eve.

WEEK 26

Reading 1

BIBLE STORY

Foreign women and their gods lead Solomon's heart astray. God's judgment on Solomon is that the kingdom will be divided.

1 Kings 11:42—12:16; 14:21–31

Why is it scary to live in a time of political turmoil where there is danger and chaos?

Why is it important to listen carefully to our parents in a time like that?

When political leaders do not respect God, why do things get crazy so quickly?

BIBLE CONVERSATION

The truth of Solomon's wisdom echoes down to this very day.

Proverbs 6:16–19

Why is it easy to *know* about good and right, but hard to *do* them?

Why are these things still bad today?

WEEK 26: READING 1

Leader Notes

David unites the kingdom. Jerusalem is on the border between the tribal territories of Judah and Benjamin. Saul is from the tribe of Benjamin, and David from Judah. The Levites have no territory but are spread throughout the tribes. The other tribes are suspicious, envious, and jealous of the tribe of Judah because they bring the center of political and religious power to their territory and God clearly affirms it.

Now they find out what a precious gift unity is. The other tribes leave the union and only Judah, Benjamin, and some Levites remain, using the temple and recognizing the king.

The relationship with God is central to all this. When the king is serving the Lord in everything he does, God lets him follow his heart's desires. But when his heart desires things that are not right, God backs away and lets him struggle on his own. This is like us in our own lives.

WEEK 26

Reading 2

BIBLE STORY

The divided kingdom of Judah and Israel spirals downward. God sends prophets to the kings of Judah and Israel.

1 Kings 16:29–34; 17

Why does Elijah have to hide after declaring a drought (1 Kings 17:3)?

Why is being the Lord's messenger sometimes hard and dangerous?

Does God guarantee that we will always be happy and comfortable if we live for him? Why?

BIBLE CONVERSATION

The widow's oil and flour do not run out. The Lord's presence with us will also go the distance.

Philippians 1:3–11

Why does Paul have joy in his prison chains?

How is having joy not the same as being comfortable or happy?

Why is joy from Jesus better than being comfortable and happy?

WEEK 26: READING 2

Leader Notes

Elijah is the greatest of Israel's prophets. He writes no book in the Bible. Prophets are God's messengers to the kings of Judah and Israel. Kings love power and they very seldom care to hear truth from God. Kings often keep false prophets who tell them what they want to hear. Prophets of the Lord are often abused, imprisoned, and killed.

Prophets of the Lord might seem a little ill-tempered in the Bible story, but not without reason. Their mission is most often to tell powerful people exactly what they do not wish to hear. Kings survive on public relations and image; being seen as strong and sure. Prophets expose their foolishness and hypocrisy. Elijah, like the prophet Jeremiah, struggles with depression and sadness, but he serves the Lord and is greatly rewarded. He does not pass through death but is taken directly into the heavens like Enoch from Genesis 5.

Paul finds the joy of the Lord Jesus in his life even though he suffers and will eventually be executed by the Romans. We live in a time and culture that demand we be happy, safe, and comfortable at all times. The amazing thing is that the wealthiest, most successful culture of all time produces great levels of worry and unhappiness. Joy is apparently found elsewhere. Study after study has confirmed that the pursuit of pleasure brings no joy at all. What consistently brings joy to humans is doing meaningful work that helps others. That is built into following and serving Jesus.

WEEK 26

Reading 3

BIBLE STORY

Elijah raises the widow's son from the dead. The Lord then sends Elijah to deal with King Ahab and the prophets of Baal.

1 Kings 18:16–46

Does seeing amazing things change people's minds forever (1 Kings 18:39)?

Why doesn't seeing a miracle make everyone do what is right so that the world is better?

What is the reason for serving the Lord and being godly?

BIBLE CONVERSATION

God's servant Elijah brings about change for Israel by his obedience. God's Son King Jesus brings about change for all the earth by his obedience.

Philippians 2:1–11

How much might God change the world around us if we live for King Jesus?

What will those of us who ignore Jesus end up doing (Philippians 2:10–11)?

WEEK 26: READING 3

Leader Notes

God is not about just obeying rules, but his rules have meaning behind them. Serving the Lord lifts us up so we can be more like our creator in whose image we are made. Serving the Baals enslaves people to drunkenness, immorality, child sacrifice, and every horrid, abusive thing a human mind can conjure, in the name of religion.

Our biggest modern idol-worshipping religion is secularism. In the name of science—a good thing—we end up worshipping ourselves and our own view of everything.

Sometimes God brings judgment to jerk things back to a better place. But God is persistent in pursuing those of us called to be his people, those who answer his call. Jesus, because of what he has done, will be the judge of all things, and rightly so. He does not simply impose something from on high. He comes and walks as one of us, lives out God's truth, is killed for it, and is now raised above all powers. We can trust that with our very lives. That is what he wants us to do, because in the end he judges his creation.

This famous passage in Philippians captures the whole gospel of Jesus emptying himself and ascending to the throne of heaven.

WEEK 27

Reading 1

BIBLE STORY

After Elijah's courageous confrontation with the prophets of Baal, he runs for his life.

1 Kings 19

Why is it okay with God for us not to be heroes every day (1 Kings 19:3–4)?

Why is lunch and a nap what we sometimes need when we are feeling low (1 Kings 19:5–7)?

Why does God twice ask Elijah, "Why are you here?"

BIBLE CONVERSATION

Like Elijah, everyone gets discouraged, but God provides comfort and joy.

Philippians 4:4–7

How do we know that our parents love us?

How do we know that God loves us and cares for us?

Why should that give us joy?

WEEK 27: READING 1

Leader Notes

After the victory at Mt. Carmel, followed by a serious death threat, Elijah is wiped out and depressed. The Lord has us live in our body and in the world. We get thrown around hard by life. Even with the amazing things Elijah sees, he must live today, and today can be hard. This does not mean that God does not care or has forgotten us.

Paul is in prison while he is writing this letter. He gets depressed and low sometimes, but he also finds the joy of the Lord. Amid that uncomfortable, temporary situation he finds joy from things that have eternal value.

WEEK 27

Reading 2

BIBLE STORY

God selects Elisha to replace Elijah, who then makes a grand exit from this life.

2 Kings 2:1–18

When we feel alone, why are we not alone (2 Kings 2:15)?

How can we relax knowing that we don't have to take care of everything God plans to do?

If we are done with something God had us do, why is it okay to move on to the next thing?

BIBLE CONVERSATION

Elisha learns everything he can from Elijah. Much later, Paul encourages the Philippians to follow his own example as well.

Philippians 4:8–9

Who is an example that you follow in this life with the Lord?

Why is it okay to be positive and to think about good things?

WEEK 27: READING 2

Leader Notes

Elijah is part of a company or school of prophets that carries the spiritual strength of Israel during the time of the kings and beyond. They are responsible for the shape of the Hebrew Bible or Old Testament we have. Their influence on us today can hardly be underestimated.

Elijah's exit from this life bypasses death. He keeps reappearing in the Bible story. He appears at the end of the prophets in Malachi's book as the one who will bring the day of the Lord. Jesus identifies John the Baptizer as Elijah. John's Gospel has people inquiring whether Jesus and John are Elijah, Moses, or the Prophet. Elijah appears with Moses on the mountain with Jesus for the inner three disciples to see before Jesus' death and resurrection. Elijah is a very important figure in identifying the Messiah.

Paul lives in an oppressive world of corruption and violence. He says to think on the goodness that God created. Being positive is not cheating or being unrealistic. It is creating space for more goodness in the world. We know and feel the effects of the evil around us, but it is God's goodness that keeps us going.

WEEK 27

Reading 3

BIBLE STORY

After Elijah is taken up, Elisha follows in his extraordinary footsteps.

2 Kings 5

What does Naaman learn about the Lord?

What should Gehazi already know about the Lord?

What does the Lord expect of us who know him?

BIBLE CONVERSATION

If Elisha speaks with God's authority, how much more God's own Son?

Colossians 1:15–18

If Jesus, the Son, is firstborn over all creation, does that mean he had a beginning?

If Jesus is over all, and head of the church, how important is the church?

Why is it so important to pay attention to the Lord, like Naaman?

WEEK 27: READING 3

Leader Notes

Naaman and Gehazi are contrasted here. Naaman, who knows only a rumor about a prophet in Samaria, is given a simple, fantastic gift. It is the servants who are the heroes here. The servant girl tells her master about the prophet. The servants convince Naaman to try the simple instructions of Elisha. It happens as the prophet says. This is a picture of simple obedient faith.

Gehazi is a different kind of picture. He has the advantage of knowing the Lord. More is expected of him. He commits a deception for personal gain. He demonstrates no faith at all. He apparently assumes the Lord does not see him. He assumes that the prophet of the Lord will not know. His lack of faith costs him very dearly. Gehazi's lack of faith is set in contrast when the prophet calls his leprosy Naaman's leprosy. The leprosy Naaman's simple faith cast away, Gehazi's lack of faith will never get rid of.

The passage from Colossians is a clear summation of the greatness of Jesus. The title of firstborn is a status in the ancient world. It often does not necessarily mean anything about the actual birth or birth order. It means that Jesus has the position of prominence in everything. It does not mean he was brought into existence. Verse 17 says that he is before all things. Other passages speak of the existence of the Son of God from eternity past.

WEEK 28

Reading 1

BIBLE STORY

Despite the amazing ministry of Elijah, Elisha, and other powerful prophets, the kings of Israel are evil, and God judges them.

2 Kings 17:1–23

Why is the Lord so patient for so long—centuries—with his people ignoring him?

Why is it unwise to test the Lord's patience?

Why is waiting until we are older to walk with God a bad idea?

BIBLE CONVERSATION

Even if our tribe is scattered, God knows where we are and cares about us.

James 1:1–8

Does having trials mean that the Lord is displeased with us? Why?

Why is struggling such an integral part of growing into a godly person?

WEEK 28: READING 1

Leader Notes

What comes to be called "Israel" in Jesus' day is mostly the tribes of Judah, Benjamin, Simeon, and a portion of the Levites. The designation of "Jewish" comes from the name Judah. The rest of the tribes exist in the form of the Samaritans, who are not considered part of Israel any longer because they are intermixed with the surrounding peoples.

The Lord is very tolerant of the northern tribes having their own capital and worship center in Samaria, wrong as it is. They will not go to Jerusalem because of intertribal envy. The Lord sends them many great prophets, but all the kings of Israel are evil. Eventually, the Lord judges them and their part in the inheritance of greater Israel is lost. Ironically, the Samaritans exist to this day as citizens of modern Israel.

James (Jacob), Jesus' brother, writes to the scattered twelve tribes. This is a different picture than Israel scattered for their sins. He is characterizing the Jewish followers of Jesus as the remnant of Israel scattered by persecution. They have not been judged by God but rather are suffering because they are his servants. Their difficulties will be profitable and advantageous to them because the Lord will use it to strengthen them, if they allow.

WEEK 28

Reading 2

BIBLE STORY

The northern kingdom of Israel is driven into exile, but in the southern kingdom of Judah some good kings come to the throne of David.

2 Kings 18:1–16

Why is it right to break up the bronze snake, a centuries-old national treasure (2 Kings 18:4)?

Why would it hard to be king of a nation that is already bound for judgment?

What good might come from us being faithful through difficult times?

BIBLE CONVERSATION

Difficulties come to good people, but God uses those if we allow.

James 1:12–18

How are trials and temptations alike? How are they different?

What does it mean that God is using us as a message to the world (James 1:18)?

What is a trial for you right now?

WEEK 28: READING 2

Leader Notes

Judah has a number of good kings, but not enough to keep them going for the long run. Hezekiah is a good king in a time when Judah's exile to Babylon is already decided. With the Lord's help he fends off the Assyrians that take Israel and receives a reprieve from the judgment until after his life is over. Hezekiah appears in 2 Kings, Isaiah, Proverbs, and both books of Chronicles.

He is like the captain of a slowly sinking ship. This is a common conundrum in the history of human politics. How does one trust the Lord through a coming historical disaster? How do believers prepare for World War II? There is immense suffering, but God uses his people to reach many lives in that time.

James speaks of growing through struggle, but also that we have a basis for this growth. We are born again, and we are firstfruits. In farming, firstfruits come as a visual sign of things to come. At the end of Passover week, the biblical holiday Firstfruits is a celebration of what God will provide based on what he had done already. The resurrection happens on the celebration of Firstfruits. Jesus is called the firstfruits of the resurrection.

WEEK 28

Reading 3

BIBLE STORY

The king of Assyria takes the cities of Judah and then demands that Jerusalem surrender.

2 Kings 18:17–30; 19:1–13, 35–37

How do God's leaders—King Hezekiah and Isaiah—help each other out in a desperate hour?

How can we know that God still cares when everything is terrible?

When the world acts boastfully to us, why should we not act that way back?

BIBLE CONVERSATION

Hezekiah lives out his faith and God rescues him. God asks that we live out our faith as well.

James 1:19–27

Why do we do good deeds, especially when things are not going well?

We see all this lived out by Jesus. Why does he want us to be this way?

Who needs looking after in our family, church, or neighborhood?

WEEK 28: READING 3

Leader Notes

Hezekiah is terrified of Assyria's armies, and rightly so. He is the last holdout against a military tsunami. He approaches the prophet Isaiah, a priest who is also part of the establishment of Jerusalem. They work together. Hezekiah is defending the temple where Isaiah is, and Isaiah speaks the words of the Lord God.

They are in a difficult place. There is no middle ground. The people will be enslaved if not slaughtered, and Hezekiah and Isaiah will be treated worse. They seek the Lord as they always have, and he makes a way forward.

James teaches very much like his brother, Jesus. He teaches a godly lifestyle that is centered in trusting the Lord. This trust means that we do not have to intimidate or cheat our way to success. We do what we should, we do all we can, and leave the rest to the Lord. We do not answer with boasting or gloating like our human nature pushes us to do.

WEEK 29

Reading 1

BIBLE STORY

After King Hezekiah comes two evil kings and then King Josiah, who follows God.

2 Kings 22

Why is God willing to act because of one person who is committed to him?

Why are leaders important for everyone?

Not everyone can be king, but what can we do ourselves?

BIBLE CONVERSATION

Josiah puts his faith into action. This is still what God requires of us.

James 2:14–26

What is the difference between trying to get into heaven by being good, and living rightly because we are already going to heaven?

We cannot fix the whole world, so where do we start making things better?

WEEK 29: READING 1

Leader Notes

Josiah brings the Scripture back into a place of prominence for his lifetime. We can only act on what is around us. Josiah is king of Judah, so he has influence there. Most of us have influence in smaller circles. God expects us to start there, usually at home. It is always easy to tell the world how it should live, but getting our own life in order seems boring and inconsequential. The problem with the world begins with each of us, and that is where Jesus starts. The solution begins with each of us.

Jesus has his people in the world to live in the same life as everyone. We have baggage, we struggle, but we are called to get our hearts right with the Lord and live for him. Our faith becomes the motivation to do right things when no one else does.

WEEK 29

Reading 2

BIBLE STORY

Despite a few good kings like Hezekiah and Josiah, the southern kingdom of Judah continues doing evil in God's eyes. Sadly, Judah is given over to the Babylonians.

2 Kings 24:18—25:21

Why are things so terrible when we give up God's protection?

If God warns about something for centuries, how patient and fair is he?

What do we know that Judah learned, since they wrote this down later, after it happened (2 Kings 24:20)?

BIBLE CONVERSATION

The exile to Babylon is terrible but not the end of the story. We always start from where we are.

James 5:13-20

Why does the Bible teach that all trouble on the earth is rooted in the human heart?

Why does the cure for trouble start with praying, singing, confessing sins, and leading one another back from the wandering we all do?

WEEK 29: READING 2

Leader Notes

This is a difficult and depressing passage that is the culmination of Israel's time in the land with judges and kings. They are on and off with God. It is so like us. When things are going well, they (and we) ignore God more and more; why do we need him? When he withdraws his protective wing, we are exposed to the wild, evil world around. It means that when things are going well, we are actively being favored by God and taking it for granted. This is directly tied to Jesus saying how difficult it is for wealthy people to enter the kingdom. God is not holding us out of his kingdom, but rather we foolishly struggle to imagine why we need him.

Elijah, from the time of the kings in Israel, is used much later in James as an example of God's patience and warning.

Following Jesus is directly related to the condition of our hearts. That is why we are not urged on toward motivational techniques or better technology. Those things can be great, but only when there is a godly heart using them.

Calling the elders to anoint with oil is not a promise of the power to heal in every instance. It is partly cultural. Olive oil was thought to have healing qualities in the ancient Mediterranean world. We still do this as an act of faith so that our hearts are open to whatever the Lord has for us.

WEEK 29

Reading 3

BIBLE STORY

While Judah is in exile, the Lord raises up Daniel and his friends, like Joseph in Egypt long before.

Daniel 1

What good was it for Daniel and friends to learn Babylonian language and literature?

What is the difference between being in the world and of the world . . . between knowing Babylonian and being Babylonian?

How might God use commitment and hard work as a young person for the rest of our life, like he used Daniel's?

BIBLE CONVERSATION

Long later, Paul instructs another godly young man, Timothy, to be faithful to his calling.

1 Timothy 4:6–10

God is with Judah in their exile, so why will he be with us when things are hard?

If Joseph, Daniel, and Timothy are young when they commit themselves to the Lord, what can stop us from being like that?

WEEK 29: READING 3

Leader Notes

Daniel is perhaps fifteen when taken into captivity. He sticks with his friends, and they all stick with the Lord. They learn the Babylonian language and culture. They are not cordoned off from the reality of their situation. They study hard, work hard, and serve the Lord with all their hearts. They stay with the Lord despite studying under pagan teachers. They are great examples of the importance of starting young and being in the world but not of the world, as the New Testament teaches (Phil 2:14–16). Daniel lives to be an old man and is a huge influence on behalf of the Lord and Israel in Babylon.

Timothy is young and takes on great responsibility working with Paul. God calls young people for his service. Parents and elders should investigate and encourage that calling.

WEEK 30

Reading 1

BIBLE STORY

Daniel and his friends are raised to positions of importance as they continue to serve God faithfully.

Daniel 3

Why is their statement, "but if not," so important (Daniel 3:18)?

When God chooses not to help us, will we serve him anyway?

Who might the mysterious fourth person in the furnace be? Is it okay if we do not exactly know?

BIBLE CONVERSATION

Just like Shadrach, Meshach, and Abednego, centuries later Timothy is a young man of godly integrity.

1 Timothy 4:11–16

Why are older people encouraged when they see young people doing the right things well?

What Scripture is Paul talking about here, since the New Testament is not yet written?

Why is that important?

WEEK 30: READING 1

Leader Notes

Daniel's three friends' statement *but if not* is saying that they are committed to the Lord no matter what happens. They are not demanding that God perform a miracle. They are saying he is able, but whatever happens, they will not worship idols. When we demand that God perform a miracle, we are testing him. He wants us to serve him, come what may.

The fourth person is a mystery. The Bible leaves this person shrouded in ambiguity, just like Melchizedek and whomever Jacob wrestled with. We know he is from God. He may be an angel from God or an embodiment of God himself. Either way, God is directly and personally involved in our lives. God gives gifts at times that we do not yet completely understand, but we get the message that he is with us and is saving us.

Timothy is commanded about the life of the young church. Its practices are carried over from the synagogue in these pagan places where the gospel is taken. The three terms in 4:13—reading, preaching, teaching—are technical terms for the synagogue services Paul grew up in and led. The fledgling church is developing its own practices from its biblical Jewish roots. They do not take their cues from the surrounding pagan religions.

WEEK 30

Reading 2

BIBLE STORY

Daniel serves in Babylon from his youth for the rest of his life. When he is an old man, he still speaks the truth, no matter who is asking the question.

Daniel 5

What do we know about Belshazzar by the fact that he drinks from the Jerusalem temple goblets (Daniel 5:23)?

Why does God let Daniel be unknown and unimportant the whole time after Nebuchadnezzar dies until Belshazzar?

What is going on during the times in life when God seems to forget about us?

BIBLE CONVERSATION

Belshazzar, though he is foolish, places great value on Daniel, who speaks the truth. The church, even more so then, ought to highly value those who speak the truth.

1 Timothy 5:17–25

Why does God ask us to cooperate and work with the leaders in our church?

What is favoritism and why is it such a natural, but wrong, part of our behavior (1 Timothy 5:21)?

What does it mean that our good deeds done in secret will not be forever hidden (1 Timothy 5:25)?

Leader Notes

Nebuchadnezzar is called Belshazzar's father. That term can mean "grandfather" or "ancestor" in this context. He is likely Belshazzar's grandfather. Daniel has been retired and forgotten, but still has important work to do. It takes a lot of courage to walk into the king's presence and speak hard truth. That is the work of a prophet.

Our lives can go long periods with nothing exciting or extraordinary happening. That does not mean God has forgotten us. God is always at work even when our everyday life seems unnoticed. Do we love our children when they are sleeping? Of course. Are they still our children when they are watching television or texting? Of course. Are they still growing, learning, and changing all that time? Of course, and so it is with God and us.

Our relationship with the leaders of our congregation is certainly different than between a king and a prophet. It is different than between government leaders and us. In public political life we express distrust in everything because we correctly assume that everyone acts in their own best interest. In the church we act with more trust because, even knowing that we all sin (1 Timothy 5:20), we know that God is working in each of us who follow Jesus. So, we seek the balance; somewhere between having foolish, blind faith in people and being cynical like we are with politicians.

WEEK 30

Reading 3

BIBLE STORY

After the death of Belshazzar, Daniel works in his old age for Darius the Mede.

Daniel 6

Why does Daniel keep praying three times a day to God?

What are some things that God asks us to do so that people see we are in his family?

What good things in our life are not negotiable—what good and right will we do no matter what?

BIBLE CONVERSATION

The same truth that saves Daniel is the word we teach today.

2 Timothy 3:14–17

When is it difficult to continue in what we have become convinced of?

Why does God give us the Bible?

Why are we to have a life-long relationship with the Bible?

Leader Notes

We live in a world where people are always laying traps for us, especially if we are doing good things. Daniel is used to the wickedness of politics, but God has been faithful his whole life. He is going to keep faith, no matter what.

Praying three times a day is more of a tradition and habit than a commandment, but it is the expression that represents Daniel's relationship with the God of Israel. Our culture is very focused on how things make us feel. This is quite opposite of God's life with us. We first do what is right and good because we are committed to it, then we might feel good about it. We do not choose what to do based only on what we feel. The Bible guides us through our lives and articulates the meaning of our relationship with God and one another so that we find joy and success in God's terms.

The Bible Paul is referring to did not yet include the New Testament. What a great treasure we now have with which to live our lives.

WEEK 31

Reading 1

BIBLE STORY

At the end of Daniel's faithful ministry some of the Israelites are allowed to go back to their land.

Ezra 1

How does God keep his people together for seventy years in a foreign place?

What remains true about us and our family over the last seventy years, good or bad?

How does God keep his people together all over the world?

BIBLE CONVERSATION

The Israelites are strangers in Babylon, and now we citizens of heaven are strangers here.

1 Peter 2:11–17

Was the Roman emperor nice to God's people in Peter's time?

Why is our worst enemy usually living right inside us (1 Peter 2:11)?

How can we be good citizens, even if government is working against us?

WEEK 31: READING 1

Leader Notes

After seventy years of exile, the foundation of what is now Israel begins to return and rebuild. Notice that the remaining tribes include only Judah, Benjamin, Simeon, and Levi. The rest are outside the community, scattered and intermarried with the Assyrians who captured them centuries before. Many Jewish people stay in Babylon. They continue and thrive until the twentieth century, when they are driven out after nearly three millennia. Great volumes of literature, the Talmud, that shaped the world of rabbinic Judaism are written over centuries in Babylon.

Daniel may well have lived to see this return begin, but he finishes out his life and work in Babylon. The articles from the temple that feature in the Belshazzar story (Daniel 5) reappear and make the trip back to Jerusalem.

In Peter's day, Rome is not friendly to anyone serving only the one God. But Jesus does not allow his disciples to imagine that the world will really change by being political rebels. It changes one heart at a time and each of us must reconcile our heart to God and allow him to change us. That is how God changes the world.

WEEK 31

Reading 2

BIBLE STORY

When some of the Israelites come back to the land, they begin by reestablishing the temple worship of God.

Ezra 3

Why do the sons of Israel start their new life in the land by rebuilding the temple and celebrating the Bible holidays (Ezra 3:2, 4)?

Why is it important to obey rules now in this part of our life, even if they will not be the rules for later in our life?

What rules apply now that may not be necessary later?

What rules might always be necessary?

BIBLE CONVERSATION

The ancient Israelites suffer in exile for their sins, and we might also, but it is better to suffer because we are committed to the Lord.

1 Peter 4:12–19

Do we need to look for ways to suffer so God will be impressed?

Why does loving God, Jesus, family, and our church bring us into conflict with the world?

What good things can happen when people oppose the good things we do?

WEEK 31: READING 2

Leader Notes

The Israelites returning are still under the law of Moses and obligated to obey it. They got sent into exile because they ignored the law. So they go back to the basics. They are no longer under the spell of power brought on by having their own king. The new temple is perhaps not as glorious as Solomon's; some old people cry when they see it. Are they crying for joy, sadness, or both? The fact that a new one even exists is miraculous.

None of the people rebuilding the temple are responsible for Israel being in exile, but they must press forward with what they have. That is often our situation. When we think of the past as glorious and now as not-so-great, it might mean that we are not seeing or hearing what God is doing. His idea of great is completely different than ours.

We go through periods where church has some popularity in the culture, and we get full of ourselves. God takes the wind out of our sails. We must be centered as followers of Jesus no matter what the situation. If we suffer for our faith, it should not be because we are self-righteous and sanctimonious. We must swim in the water with everyone else. God has called us to be his influence in the world, and that will sometimes cost us.

WEEK 31

Reading 3

BIBLE STORY

After the Israelites re-establish the worship of God in Jerusalem, they look again into his word. A new kind of worship happens that we still practice today.

Nehemiah 7:73b- 8:18

Why is meeting in the open easier than in the temple (Nehemiah 8:2)?

In what ways does this meeting seem like church today?

Why is it amazing that we all now have Bibles?

BIBLE CONVERSATION

Ezra the priest leads the returnees, and the church is led by its elders.

1 Peter 5:1–11

How is Jesus our example in taking care of one another?

Why is being in charge more about being responsible than telling people what to do?

What kinds of things are you responsible for right now?

WEEK 31: READING 3

Leader Notes

This meeting to read the Scripture is an amazing milestone in the Bible. Everything that the synagogue and the church become flows out of this event. There are no restrictions of birth like the temple (priest, Levite, Israelite, man, woman, gentile). Whoever can understand comes to listen.

The process of expositional preaching is rooted in Nehemiah 8:8 where the Bible teachers are explaining what the text means for people trying to understand. That is huge. From this process eventually come the apostles who proclaim Jesus and teach his Scripture.

Peter reminds believers that we all have a shepherd. Jesus is our Chief Shepherd to whom we will answer. "Pastor" means "shepherd." Pastors and elders are the same thing in the church. Pastors are elders who teach. Leadership is about being responsible and taking care of something. The power of being boss can be irresistible, but that is where Jesus' example is so important. He has all power, but he lets people make choices, then and now.

WEEK 32

Reading 1

BIBLE STORY

After many centuries and generations, the promised Seed of Abraham, the Son of David, is born into the world of humans.

Matthew 1

Why is it important to have a genealogy, to know who Jesus is?

Why is it important that Joseph and Mary are good, righteous people?

Why is it so amazing that God is with us, as one of us?

BIBLE CONVERSATION

Israel has been thinking about important sons for a long time. Now Immanuel is here.

Isaiah 7:10–14

Judah's King Ahaz pretends to not want to test the Lord, but he does. How?

If God offers us something, why should we trust him by taking it?

Why should we get close, and stay close, to Immanuel (Jesus)?

WEEK 32: READING 1

Leader Notes

Matthew writes to a Jewish audience and emphasizes what will make sense to them about this Jewish Messiah, Jesus. Our western mind, shaped by science and technology, struggles to see the way a literary device like a genealogy is used. Matthew starts his Gospel connecting Jesus to David and Abraham. The genealogy is not used like we would use it. It can skip generations and take literary artforms to make its point. For example, in 1:17, the word "fourteen" also spells "David" in Hebrew. There are other numeric design features. It is perfectly legitimate, even clever, in the ancient world to connect Jesus to David in that way.

The message of the genealogy is that Jesus is legitimate in every way. He is the one for whom we have waited, so don't hesitate.

Joseph and Mary (Yosef and Miriam) are upstanding Jewish working people. Matthew presents Joseph's perspective in his birth story and Luke presents Mary's. By the time these things are written down, only Mary is still alive to tell the story. It is their commitment to the God of Israel that gets Joseph and Mary through the stress of this situation. In this era, an unaccounted-for pregnancy can be extremely serious business.

Isaiah is talking about a current situation in Judah but reaches forward to show where God is taking this. God himself will enter the human race—unthinkable—but that is the foundation of the gospel.

WEEK 32

Reading 2

BIBLE STORY

Bethlehem, the hometown of David, is where everything begins again for the new King of Israel.

Luke 2:1–20

How does God use politics to get Joseph and Mary to Bethlehem?

Why does God enter humanity in the middle of a mess?

Why does God put poor people and shepherds in his story?

BIBLE CONVERSATION

This place of beginning again is long foretold by the ancient prophets of Israel. King David, shepherd of Israel, begins here as a shepherd. His descendant King Jesus begins shepherding Israel and all creation from among the shepherds of Bethlehem.

Micah 5:2–4 (5:1–3 in Hebrew text)

Why is God always able to surprise us by starting with humble beginnings?

What does that say about us?

How is being a shepherd a picture of God caring for us?

WEEK 32: READING 2

Leader Notes

Joseph and Mary are in an extremely difficult situation. There is a lot of social and political pressure on them. Many marriages and engagements do not survive that kind of pressure. They are deeply committed to doing the right thing. God chooses well, no surprise.

Jesus' beginnings in our flesh have some tremendous lessons and encouragements for us. Don't look to the great trappings of state and church for the thing that is really happening. God loves all of us and is not one bit intimidated by our social structures. He knows they are often an illusory, unstable house of cards that we create for ourselves.

God does not have to work hard to surprise most of us. We always fall for the same things. We are easily entertained by bright, shiny objects, while the truth is going on elsewhere. Who thinks a baby born in a cave to two poor people is going to be important?

Micah's prophecy is important in Jesus' day. Being born in Bethlehem in the line of David is a key messianic marker for those who study Scripture. However, being from the line of Judah (even David) or Bethlehem are not rare things. There are many people born in Bethlehem over the centuries. Most of the people in Israel after the exile to Babylon are now from the tribe of Judah, Benjamin, or Levi. There is much more prophecy, but this is the starting place to identify the Messiah.

The chapter and verse numberings in the Hebrew Bible are a bit different in some places, and some English translations in the Christian world now reflect that.

WEEK 32

Reading 3

BIBLE STORY

From Bethlehem the hometown of David, to Jerusalem the city of David, comes this baby who is the son of David. Jesus is a son of his people Israel, Jewish in every way from start to finish. That is central to understanding the gospel.

Luke 2:21–40

Why is Joseph and Mary's poor-person offering (a dove) just as meaningful to God as the offering of a wealthier person (a lamb)?

Why is it critical to do the right thing now even though we don't yet understand it all (Luke 2:33)?

BIBLE CONVERSATION

The principle of the firstborn belonging to God is at the center of the Passover story, the Law of Moses, and the Messiah Jesus.

Exodus 13:1–3, 14–15

Why is it important to God that we always ask the question "What does this mean?" for the rest of our lives?

Why would Jesus later be called the Lamb of God who takes away the sins of the world?

How are our lives protected by the blood of the lamb, Jesus?

Leader Notes

Joseph and Mary bring the required sacrifice to redeem their firstborn son at the temple in Jerusalem. In Leviticus either a lamb or a dove is required. The dove is given in place of a lamb if a person is not able to afford a lamb. The lamb is certainly more expensive, but does it represent a bigger sacrifice? Jesus later points out the couple of coins that a widow puts in the treasury and notes that her sacrifice is greater than the expensive gifts of the wealthy (Luke 21:1–4). It is a greater sacrifice because she needs that money to live on. So, the dove is not a lesser sacrifice; it might be greater. Joseph and Mary do not yet understand the significance of their child, but they keep doing the right thing and it is revealed as their lives go on.

The firstborn of anyone in the first Passover is saved from death by the blood of the lamb that is slain. Its blood is put on the doorposts of the house of every family. Israel shelters under the blood of the lamb and Egypt does not. Even so, there are some Egyptians who shelter under the blood and leave with Israel. It is not about ethnicity; it is about trusting God and obeying him. After the exodus from Egypt, God requires that all firstborns be redeemed, and so with Jesus. Jesus is the Lamb of God whose shed blood saves and protects from coming judgment. That is the foundation of the gospel.

WEEK 33

Reading 1

BIBLE STORY

Jesus comes as rightful king and that threatens lesser kings. Jesus comes up out of Egypt like Israel.

Matthew 2

Why are kings always threatened by other people who might become king?

If Jesus' parents—important people—are told to run for their lives, how does God protect us?

How is God involved in our lives in crazy times, and then when nothing seems to be happening?

BIBLE CONVERSATION

Matthew quotes a long-ago prophet who is looking back to the Law and the first exodus. This new exodus that Jesus leads makes a way out of our human slavery to sin.

Hosea 11:1-4

How do parents teach their children to walk?

How much do parents love their children?

How does Jesus show us God's love for us?

WEEK 33: READING 1

Leader Notes

Herod is cast in Matthew's Gospel as another Pharaoh. He kills the baby boys to stop God. Jesus escapes Herod as Moses escaped Pharaoh.

The quote from Jeremiah is originally referring to the place, Ramah, where the Babylonians did their deportations, taking the young and skilled leaders of Judah—like Daniel and friends—away into exile forever. Rachel here is a representation of Jewish mothers mourning the loss of their children to Pharaoh in Egypt, Nebuchadnezzar in Babylon, and now Herod. Jesus, the seed of Eve, comes into the hostile world and is attacked by the seed of the snake mentioned in Genesis 3:15. The war between the seed of the woman and the seed of the serpent continues.

Jesus is protected not by magic but by knowledge: *Someone is trying to harm you*. Joseph is warned to flee—*Go to Egypt until you are told to come back*. He has no insurance, no credit card, and no safety net. This is a big clue in how we relate to God. His protection over us may involve us having the wisdom and strength to escape and to endure difficulty. We always hope for a situation that keeps us safe and comfortable, but God knows we do not grow that way. We struggle and keep our eyes and ears open to what God is doing.

Matthew exegetes Hosea, who is exegeting Numbers 23 and 24. The exodus from Egypt becomes a picture of the return from exile in Hosea's time, and finally Jesus coming out of Egypt as the King of Israel (Numbers 24:8).

WEEK 33

Reading 2

BIBLE STORY

Jesus grows up and lives in the center of his people Israel. He listens, asks questions, answers questions, and walks between Galilee and Jerusalem his entire life.

Luke 2:41–51

How big might the group of family and friends be walking home from Jerusalem, so that Jesus is not missed for a whole day?

Why, perhaps, are twelve-year-olds allowed to be so independent in the ancient world?

If our parents come looking for us, what will they most likely to find us doing?

BIBLE CONVERSATION

Jesus is the living embodiment of all that God intends in the Law of Moses.

Psalm 119:17–20

What is the difference between being a rule-keeper and "being consumed with longing for your laws?"

How can my relationship with the Lord "open my eyes to wonderful things in his law?" What things?

How are we able to be close with God, whatever part of life we are in?

WEEK 33: READING 2

Leader Notes

People tend to stay with friends and extended family for safety in the ancient world. The threat of being put out of one's family and community is terrifying and dangerous. Personal autonomy is a relatively modern phenomenon. People take their personal identity from family, tribe, neighborhood, and village. We still do but not nearly as deeply.

Jesus walks from the Galilee to Jerusalem for the holidays with family and friends one to three times a year his entire life. The Psalms of Ascent (120–34) are written just for that journey.

Jesus is special from the beginning, but what that means is not completely clear to anyone, especially his parents. God takes on flesh and lives with all the confinements of being one of us. That is much easier for us to see in retrospect, especially with the Holy Spirit giving understanding and inspiring the eyewitnesses to write down Scripture.

It is important to live out what and where we are in life. When we are young, we are often consumed with the idea of being older. When we get older, we spend our lives trying to look and act younger. There are modes of learning when we are young that are not as easy or even possible as we get older. There are things we cannot yet process when we are young. There should always be a sense of growing wonder and amazement at what God is doing in us and others. Jesus is fully part of this developmental growing-up, changing process. He is special, but he is one of us.

WEEK 33

Reading 3

BIBLE STORY

When Jesus is about thirty years old, the time comes for him to be introduced to his people. His cousin John comes as Elijah announcing the Day of the Lord and then baptizes Jesus.

Matthew 3

Why does God have Jesus introduced out in the desert where hardly anyone lives?

Why is John not nice to the powerful people in charge?

Why does John not want to baptize Jesus?

BIBLE CONVERSATION

John's call to repentance is a culmination of the Hebrew prophetic writings.

Isaiah 1:1–4, 18

Why is the relationship of the Lord with his own people so important to him?

Why is everyone in the same trouble with God as ancient Israel?

How does Jesus make it possible for everyone's scarlet sins to be white as snow?

WEEK 33: READING 3

Leader Notes

John the Baptizer brings a baptism of repentance, not unlike the cleansing bath (*mikveh*) that Jewish people already practice. John's baptism is a way of saying, "I want to be right with God, and I know I don't deserve to stand before him. I want whatever he has for me." John is described in the same way as the ancient prophet Elijah (Matthew 3:4). Later, after John's imprisonment, Jesus will directly say that John is Elijah (Matthew 11:14).

In keeping with his prophetic role, John calls out the religious leadership for their hypocrisy and corruption. Jesus does the same. This does not go down well with the leaders, as it seldom does.

Jesus has John baptize him. John knows that Jesus has no sin to repent of, but Jesus makes a milestone transition of it. Here the Father speaks, the Son is identified, and the Holy Spirit appears. Jesus is affirmed by God in no uncertain terms and begins his ministry.

The problem of sin is *the* problem since the garden. Jesus is the great deliverance foreshadowed by the exodus, the return from exile, and so much else. Centuries before Jesus, the prophet Isaiah lays out the problem with stark clarity. He also clearly foretells God's coming as a righteous servant, suffering on behalf of the sins of his people and for all humankind.

WEEK 34

Reading 1

BIBLE STORY

After baptism, the Holy Spirit leads Jesus into the desert to finish some old business between the devil and mankind. Jesus' public ministry begins from here.

Matthew 4:1–17

The devil and Jesus both quote Scripture; why is that important?

How did Adam and Eve fail in the garden?

How did Israel fail in the desert (Hint: *mooo*)?

Why is it important that Jesus succeeds as an Israelite and as a human being?

BIBLE CONVERSATION

God begins to bring about the fulfillment of all things through his son Jesus.

Isaiah 2:1–4

To what kind of greatness is Jesus leading us?

Jesus was tempted. If we have no difficulties, only good circumstances, how does that help us have right hearts?

If God changes our heart, how might that change our life?

Leader Notes

Adam and Eve—representing all humanity—fail in perfect circumstances, a garden with God. Israel fails while God is feeding them from his hand in the desert. Jesus—representing Israel and all humanity—comes and wins this battle for us while starving in the desert.

God takes on flesh, so the victories he wins in the flesh, he wins for us, as one of us. It is better than having a major league professional baseball player bat on our little league team.

Isaiah brings us to the final great picture, the mountain of the Lord. It is the redemption of Israel and humanity, the reconciliation of all that is lost and broken. That is where God is taking us, but how will he achieve this? God chooses those who choose him. He changes the world one heart at a time. He comes and shows us what that looks like, in Jesus.

We want to have everything easy, but God knows it does not help us. By changing us inside first, our new lives begin to make better circumstances all around us.

WEEK 34

Reading 2

BIBLE STORY

After the temptation in the wilderness, Jesus begins his public ministry at his hometown synagogue. Home can be the hardest place to start.

Luke 4:16–44

Why does our mind think that we, and no one else, are special (Luke 4:28–29)?

Why do we have a hard time believing what the demons already know (Luke 4:33–34)?

How do we know that we sometimes need to rest (Luke 4:42)?

BIBLE CONVERSATION

When God takes on flesh, Jesus, it should be easier for us to respond to him. Humans meeting God face-to-face is always a problem.

Isaiah 6:1–8

Why is God so terrifying?

What do we always forget that Isaiah standing before God immediately understands (Isaiah 6:5)?

What does it mean for us to say, like Isaiah, "Here am I Lord. Send me?"

WEEK 34: READING 2

Leader Notes

Jesus goes home to Nazareth, where he has been in synagogue since childhood. Our hometown can hardly ever imagine us being more than we were as a child. It is a universal human phenomenon. He ups the ante by proclaiming that he is the fulfillment of Isaiah's prophecy. That is an extremely bold statement that will fade quickly away unless he backs it up, which he does many times. They are struggling to make the simple connection between Jesus' miracles and this passage.

Jesus builds up the pressure on their unbelief by mentioning the outreach of Elijah and Elisha to gentiles. The implication is pointed—God responds to whomever seeks him. They are not ready to hear this. The exile centuries ago, taught them not to be idol worshippers. Now they cannot imagine that God would reach out in love to idol worshippers. They get violent.

Isaiah's vision of the Lord in the temple brings Luke's passage into contrast. People are impossible to convince. The vision terrifies Isaiah, and he understands that he should not be alive before this Holy God. Centuries before Isaiah, the Israelites ask Moses to deal with God in their place because they are terrified. So, God takes on human flesh, in part, to soften the terror. Then we humans are not impressed: "Aren't you Joseph's son?" Even with miracles, we are not convinced. Only those who are called are convinced; it is a minority called in the Bible, a remnant. It is a common human thought that if we could just see a miracle, we would believe. But the whole Bible story stands against that notion.

WEEK 34

Reading 3

BIBLE STORY

In Jesus' public ministry he reaches out to all levels of society, even the top.

John 3:1–21

Why do we know that Nicodemus was on the right track (John 3:2)?

Why does God want us to be born of the Spirit?

Why have so many millions of people memorized John 3:16? Have you?

BIBLE CONVERSATION

God always makes his message clear to everyone who will listen and seek him.

Isaiah 8:19–22

How many voices are speaking to us from all our machines (computer, phone, TV, etc.)?

What is the main way we hear God's voice (Isaiah 8:20)?

What has God been speaking about to you lately?

Leader Notes

John 3 begins a series of encounters that Jesus has with three different kinds of people: a Jewish man from the ruling council (Nicodemus), a Samaritan woman, and a gentile. John arranges these stories together to make a point that Jesus is reaching out to everyone. Nicodemus understands the basic truth about Jesus: *These miracles mean that you are from God.* Nicodemus is violating all his world's social norms by coming to Jesus to seek and listen. Nicodemus shows up later and may well have become part of the community of believers.

Jesus speaks about being born again, and Nicodemus is incredulous. It does not fit the traditional understanding that has gone on for centuries. It is something new that Jesus is bringing. Spiritual rebirth is in the Law and the Prophets but always coming later. Jesus is now making it readily available. That is amazing and world-changing!

Isaiah lives in a time when people are worshipping idols and seeking spiritual guidance from cultic sources. The Lord is skeptical of their inquiries; why consult the dead on behalf of the living? God gives insight into the spirit realm in his word, through his Spirit, and through his prophets. We avoid God's truth. We often seek out darkness because we think we can hide there. God wants us to bring everything out into the light. That feels far too revealing.

WEEK 35

Reading 1

BIBLE STORY

After Jesus shares with Nicodemus from the ruling council, he shares with a Samaritan woman and a gentile as well.

John 4:1–26, 39–54

What does Jesus mean by never thirsting again (John 4:14)?

Why does Jesus tell the Samaritan woman that he is the Messiah when he tells no one in Israel (John 4:26)?

How can we worship in spirit and in truth (John 4:23)?

BIBLE CONVERSATION

The gospel going to the gentiles should not be a complete surprise to anyone.

Isaiah 9:1–7

If God spends so much time telling Israel not to be like the gentiles, why will he bring the gentiles into the people of God?

How many things are we unable to hear because they do not fit with what we already know?

How will it be to see Jesus as the King, which he is now?

WEEK 35: READING 1

Leader Notes

Jesus' conversation with the Samaritan woman dives headlong into ancient tribal disputes. The Samaritans are the remainder of the other Israelite tribes besides Judah, Benjamin, Simeon, and Levi. They had intermarried and were out of the nation. This ancient rivalry went back to Jacob's declaration of blessing to the tribes in Genesis 49. There were two heroes, Judah and Joseph. They were both rewarded but all these centuries later Judah has won out. The term "Jewish" refers to the name of Judah. Joseph, or his son Ephraim, come to represent the lost tribes taken by the Assyrians, later called Samaritans. The Samaritan woman's bitterness shows in her conversation with Jesus.

Jesus declares that even though God chooses Judah to carry forth his plan to the Messiah, he regards all humans equally made in his image and will save all who come to him. Isaiah tells of Jesus reigning on David's throne. Jesus is Jewish and will always be so; God's promises all stand. He will, though, bless all who come to worship and serve.

It is difficult for us to take in the meaning of new things when they appear. God is making real change but has foretold it clearly. We struggle to hear new things; they do not fit into our picture of life. In that day when we see the Lord there will be many surprises that should have been clear to us, but we just won't see it.

WEEK 35

Reading 2

BIBLE STORY

As Jesus begins his public ministry, he chooses twelve disciples.

Luke 5:1–11, 27–39; 6:12–16

What other Bible group has twelve leaders?

Why does it seem unlikely that Jesus will change the world with twelve guys?

What things do you feel unqualified to do that God says you can do?

BIBLE CONVERSATION

Jesus' unassuming, unnoticed start will culminate in greatness like the world has never seen.

Isaiah 11:1–9

What good things has modern science brought to the world (health, wealth, etc.)?

How much of that happened because people lived in the light of God, Jesus, and the Bible?

What good things has science not brought? What are we waiting for from God?

Why do we need God?

Leader Notes

Jesus chooses twelve disciples like there are twelve tribes of Israel. Jesus is a picture of Israel. He represents Israel and he represents humanity just like he does in the temptation.

Jesus heals and feeds thousands of people, but he is not a national healthcare or welfare provider. Most of the people who see or receive miraculous things do not keep following. It is easy to make the case that Jesus' whole ministry is mostly done so that these twelve (minus Judas Iscariot) will believe all the way through the crucifixion, to the resurrection, and to the giving of the Holy Spirit. He invests in his own people.

Centuries earlier Isaiah paints the picture of this king coming from the house of Jesse. The vision of the whole earth being filled with the knowledge of the Lord is carried forward by Jesus and then his people.

Modern science comes to fruition and flourishes in the soil of a biblical worldview. It makes the world better in many ways. Life expectancy nearly doubles in the last two centuries. In 1900 80 percent of the world is in dire poverty, now 12%. The common person lives better than kings of old. But the human heart remains unchanged. Technology amplifies human desires for good and for ill. We do far greater good and far greater evil with our technology. We need the Lord to continue changing the hearts of humans one by one until he returns.

WEEK 35

Reading 3

BIBLE STORY

On the mountain with his followers, like Moses at Mt. Sinai, Jesus teaches about the law and being God's Kingdom-of-Heaven people.

Matthew 5:1–20; 6:5–15, 25–34

Why does Jesus tell disadvantaged people that God is working in the world through their difficulties?

Why is that the best news ever?

What are the most important things to God about our lives (Matthew 6:31–34)?

BIBLE CONVERSATION

Jesus' teaching lays the foundation for the future on a mountain that God reveals long before.

Isaiah 25:6–9

Why do people think that following Jesus is foolish?

How will being a follower of Jesus mean something different when God swallows up death (Isaiah 25:7–8)?

Can we trust God to bring that day for us?

WEEK 35: READING 3

Leader Notes

Matthew writes using forms that his Jewish audience will recognize. We have seen Herod cast as Pharaoh, John as Elijah, and now Jesus as Moses. This is important because, in the minds of the people listening to the Sermon on the Mount, no one was more important than Moses. They struggle to see Jesus in that league, but he is actually much greater. We know that looking back, but when it is happening it is extremely difficult to see. If Americans have a president they like, they might think, "Well, he's doing alright, but he's no George Washington." Moses leaves big shoes to fill.

Jesus teaches that their lives as Jewish poor people have meaning in God's kingdom. They have been taught that their poverty and sickness is because they or their parents are sinners and cursed by God. Jesus' authoritative words, backed up by miracles, break through the fog of oppression they live in.

The disgrace of trusting a God we cannot see has always been carried by the Lord's people. Long ago Isaiah sees the end of all things, where the Lord Almighty brings all things to a close and describes it as removing the disgrace of his people. It is not gloating or rejoicing over others, but simply walking out from under the shroud of death and into God's *life*. That is what following Jesus will mean for those who walk with him all their lives.

WEEK 36

Reading 1

BIBLE STORY

In keeping with his teaching, Jesus demonstrates that God is not afraid of being made unclean by gentiles or the dead.

Luke 7:1–35

The Gospels say that Jesus is amazed only a couple of times; why here at verse nine?

Why is Jesus not worried about being made unclean by touching a dead person?

Why is it easy, but wrong, to find any excuse not to follow the Lord (Luke 7:31–35)?

BIBLE CONVERSATION

Despite our perceived need for religious forms, God is moving us towards his unfettered joy.

Isaiah 35

How does Jesus fit this description (especially verses 5–6) of how God saves those who love him?

How has John the Baptizer, now in prison, cleared the way for Jesus?

How do we get to share in this joy?

WEEK 36: READING 1

Leader Notes

The stone foundation of the ancient synagogue at Capernaum still exists, holding up a reconstructed foundation of a later time. The centurions in the Gospels and Acts are well spoken of here at Capernaum, at the cross saying "Surely this was the Son of God." In Acts we meet centurions Cornelius and Julius, who are shown in a positive way.

Jesus draws crowds because he heals. He touches lepers, and here a dead body, without fear of being made unclean. Cleanness is flowing from him into the person being healed or resurrected.

Jesus' statement about John the Baptizer cuts to the heart of people who like religion but do not really engage with God. We are fickle, like Goldilocks: "John is too intense, and Jesus is too relational." Our human nature reinvents God in our own image and holds him off at a safe distance. We ignore him, but he is not safe to ignore.

WEEK 36

Reading 2

BIBLE STORY

Being a follower of Jesus, a disciple, means continuing with him to find out what his truth means.

Luke 8:1–15

Why does Luke mention the many women following Jesus?

How do we get to know the meaning of the parable if we live in that day (Luke 8:9)?

How is the seed from the parable taking root in your heart?

BIBLE CONVERSATION

In the Bible, seeds represent the possibility of future things, even during judgment and trouble.

Isaiah 6:9–13

How is the passage that Jesus quotes still true today for all of us?

Why is it important that the seed is alive, though it may not look like it?

Why do we hope for things we cannot see?

WEEK 36: READING 2

Leader Notes

Women are largely unnoticed in that world, even though they are a huge part of the Bible story. Luke especially lets us know that women are central in the Gospels and Acts.

The disciples here are more than the Twelve. They are whoever follows Jesus. They distinguish themselves from the crowds by staying close to Jesus when everyone else goes home. They stay close and ask more questions. Jesus gives them answers that he does not give to the crowds who come only to get healing, food, see what is going on, or be entertained.

The Isaiah passage that Jesus quotes is about seeds as well. Here the tree cut down leaves a stump that will grow the next tree from God. It looks dead, but it is alive.

WEEK 36

Reading 3

BIBLE STORY

Jesus tells parables that are mysteries to those who want only entertainment. But to those who must know, the parables are a great new picture of what God is like.

Matthew 13:24-52

Why is it important that we live in our dark world so that we shine bright as the sun (Matthew 13:29-30, 43)?

How valuable is being part of God's kingdom compared to our favorite video games?

Why is it important to always stay close to Jesus (Matthew 13:36, 51-52)?

BIBLE CONVERSATION

The deep truths of God take our lifetime to appreciate. That is why he wants us to start thinking, praying, and living for him while we are children.

Psalm 78:1-7

In an age where we know many things, why is so important to understand what God says these things mean?

Why is it a great joy to have a lifetime ahead to learn more about the Lord's love for us?

What do we do if we don't hear God's truth until we are older?

WEEK 36: READING 3

Leader Notes

Matthew organizes his Gospel into teaching and action sections. This teaching section brings parables together. These parables are all about the nature of the kingdom of God. These were new ideas to the disciples. We have had them for two thousand years and still marvel at their insight. The great truth in the parables is that God comes to where we live. They are everyday examples of eternal truth. Even if we don't start until late in life, God meets us where we are.

The separation of the crowds and the disciples is important. The crowds always check things out to see if there is anything they can get lucky about today. It is like how people buy lottery tickets hoping all their dreams will come true but knowing they won't. The disciples stay close; they eat and sleep wherever Jesus is. They find out what he really means.

If this truth has eternal value, we are responsible to pass it on to our children. Everything else we do—career, education, etc.—is for our lifetime. But teaching our children is for the future.

WEEK 37

Reading 1

BIBLE STORY

Beyond the big surprise that he cares about gentiles and can heal at a distance, Jesus opens the disciples' eyes even further.

Luke 8:19–39

Is Jesus making his family less important, or emphasizing the importance of following him (Luke 8:19–21)?

Are the disciples more afraid of the storm or who is in the boat with them? Why?

Why does our relationship with Jesus include respect and awe?

BIBLE CONVERSATION

The amazing things God does should not surprise us.

Job 38:1–7

If God creates everything we see or imagine, is anything too hard for him?

Why does understanding more about creation make God more amazing?

WEEK 37: READING 1

Leader Notes

Jesus is not lowering the status of his own blood family. He takes care of his mother from the cross (John 19:25–27) and appears to his unbelieving brother after the resurrection (1 Corinthians 15:7). His point is that those born again are his spirit family and are tied to him forever.

In this same storm-on-the-lake story in Mark 4:41, the disciples who think they are going to drown from the storm are terrified that Jesus calms the storm. One of the weaknesses of being human is that we bring everything down to our own level. When God comes to Mt. Sinai in Exodus 19, the Israelites are so terrified they ask Moses to deal with God for them. They want someone to whom they can complain and with whom they can argue. So, God comes in human flesh—Jesus—but other humans can't believe that he is anything special. Then when they catch a glimpse of his reality, they are back to being terrified.

WEEK 37

Reading 2

BIBLE STORY	**BIBLE CONVERSATION**
Jesus shows himself master of the weather and of spirits, then he shows himself master over death itself.	Long before Jesus shows us God, Job discovers that God is master over everything.
Luke 8:40–56	**Job 40:1–14**
In the story, does everyone in the crowd who bumps into Jesus get healed? Why this woman?	If Jesus raises the dead, who is he really?
Will the girl raised from the dead have to die again? How is that different than Jesus' resurrection?	If he creates and gives life, can he also destroy and take life?
What are some of the ways Jesus gives life?	Why is it important not to live life ignoring God?

WEEK 37: READING 2

Leader Notes

Jesus does miracles that increasingly show that he is not just a teaching Rabbi who can heal. He slowly reveals to his disciples the true nature of who they are with. He is preparing them for their greatest test as followers, seeing him crucified. How great is his power over death? He heals others, can he heal himself? That depends on who he really is.

If Jesus is who his disciples are beginning to suspect he is, what does this mean? It means that the man sharing supper with them is the same Lord who speaks out of the storm to Job.

WEEK 37

Reading 3

BIBLE STORY

After Jesus raises the synagogue leader's daughter from the dead, he shows himself master over the Sabbath.

John 5:1–18

Is the man, by carrying his mat, breaking the Law of Moses or the traditions about the Law of Moses?

Why does Jesus heal this man?

Why does he care about you and me?

BIBLE CONVERSATION

The man at the pool has been there thirty-eight years. God knows how long our suffering has gone on and everything else about us.

Psalm 139:1–18

How long has God known about us?

How much does he care about us?

How does Jesus show us how much God cares about us?

WEEK 37: READING 3

Leader Notes

The lame man is trapped by a fable that when an angel stirs the water, the next person to get in the water will be healed. He thinks things can never change. The religious leaders are trapped by their own history of traditions about what constitutes work on the Sabbath. They stay trapped because those traditions give them power. Jesus breaks through both of those things. Our perceptions and reality are often not the same things.

The question becomes, if Jesus is from God, or is God, is God allowed to heal on the Sabbath? And is he breaking the law by breaking the tradition concerning the law? The leaders certainly do not think Jesus is the Messiah or the Son of God. So, for them this is someone defying their authority. The larger, more dangerous question growing is, Who is Jesus?

David's psalm breaks through the barriers that our need for control creates. David lives under the law and understands its value but is not as entrapped by a tradition of interpretation as a thousand years later when Jesus lives. He develops theological thinking out of the glory of creation, which is the beginning of the Law of Moses.

WEEK 38

Reading 1

BIBLE STORY

Jesus shows himself master over all the uncontrollable things in the disciples' lives. He then brings them to a new level of commitment to himself.

John 6:1-21, 57-69

Why do the people want to make Jesus king (John 6:15)? Why does Jesus leave them because of that?

Why are they all leaving him a short time later (John 6:66)?

What do you think: Is Jesus the king?

BIBLE CONVERSATION

The things most people desire—food and good health—turn out to be far less than what God has for us.

Isaiah 40:1-8

How does Jesus comfort us?

How does John the Baptizer prepare the way for the glory of the Lord?

What does it mean that our lives are grass?

WEEK 38: READING 1

Leader Notes

John 6:14 is a reference to Deuteronomy 18:15 about God sending another prophet like Moses. The people want him to be king because he gives them food and healing. Jesus gets away from them to stop that from happening. They are right for the wrong reason. He is king because he is the Son of God. He did not come to bring welfare and healthcare. His miracles are simply a sign that God is here right now, and we should listen to him.

Jesus, later in chapter 6, tells the crowds that they are seeking another meal. He says that they should consume his flesh and blood. That offends them because they are taking it wrong. Jesus knows this. He is offending them because they don't want to see. This is parallel to his statement that you must be born again. They are spiritual sayings with spiritual meanings because physically eating his flesh and blood is disgusting, like being born again is physically impossible.

Jesus' twelve disciples are the last ones remaining after his offensive words drive everyone else away. They have seen more than anyone in the crowds has seen. Peter gets that they are with the Messiah and says so. Peter's words are dangerous in that world and will eventually bring about the death of Jesus and Peter.

Isaiah begins a major section that include what are called the servant songs. These culminate in the death of the righteous servant (who turns out to be Jesus) on behalf of his people. This section of Isaiah is a central piece of messianic prophecy.

WEEK 38

Reading 2

BIBLE STORY

The disciples decide to follow Jesus when everyone else leaves. They learn about the cost of following him, and then see with their eyes what they believe in their hearts.

Luke 9:18–36

Why is it important for Peter, James, and John to see Jesus in his heavenly form before they see him dead on a Roman cross?

Why are the most important things in life often so scary?

How much more is there about Jesus that the disciples have not yet seen?

BIBLE CONVERSATION

The disciples' glimpse of glory confirms again that Jesus is from God.

Isaiah 40:12–17

Does God worry about what powerful kings and armies will do?

Does he care about what happens to us when we get caught in bad times?

What does he give us to go through the worst storms in life?

WEEK 38: READING 2

Leader Notes

Jesus knows that when the world system, represented by Israel's leaders and the Romans, condemns and kills him, his followers will be shattered and scattered. They will run for their lives, with good reason. They need to see this heavenly reality now to have a place to return to after the coming trauma. Jesus' resurrection will make the difference, but his horrifying death will not be easy to shake off even so. They will hardly remember his prediction or be able to imagine a resurrection after what they see.

Isaiah reminds us whom we serve, even in the midst of traumatizing circumstances. In Isaiah's time Israel is being conquered and deported. Will they remember God? In the Gospels, Jesus is going to be crucified. Will they remember what they saw on the mountain? God gives the hope we need for the difficult things coming our way.

WEEK 38

Reading 3

BIBLE STORY

On the last walk to Jerusalem with his disciples, Jesus continues to take away all our excuses for treating one another poorly.

Luke 10:25–42

Why are some people easy not to like?

Why is Jesus trying to get us to love them?

Do we have to like or trust enemies that we forgive and treat humanely?

BIBLE CONVERSATION

Since the beginning, the Lord gives plenty of examples of how to care for one another. He means for us to find many other ways to love one another.

Leviticus 19:9–18

Why is Jesus' teaching such a surprise since it has been in Scripture all along?

Why do we avoid doing things we don't want to do?

How do we love ourselves (Leviticus 19:18)?

WEEK 38: READING 3

Leader Notes

Our nature is to categorize people as *us* or *them*. We do that to survive. Some people are dangerous to us or our family. We are responsible for keeping our family safe. But our nature is such that we quickly use that responsibility as an excuse to ignore the needs of others. Jesus is asking us to take a chance on others, in the same way he takes a chance with us.

We are to love our neighbors as ourselves. We wash, feed, and care for our own bodies. We should do that for others. There are some others for which that is difficult. Jesus is not nice to everyone. He is intentionally tough on those who only give in order to receive.

Jesus is not saying anything new. The Law urges us this direction while also trying to keep us from being outright wicked.

WEEK 39

Reading 1

BIBLE STORY

As Jesus makes his way to Jerusalem for his final Passover, the pressure mounts, but he is even more determined.

Luke 13:22–35

Why is it scary for the twelve disciples and other followers to hear Jesus say these things?

What does it mean that all the people in the story, Jesus, his followers, and his enemies (except Herod) are Jewish?

Why is the choice about following Jesus so important?

BIBLE CONVERSATION

As the ancient priests welcome their king, so will all Israel someday welcome their King of Kings!

Psalm 118:19–26

How is Jesus a surprise, like the rejected stone that turns out to be the chief cornerstone?

Why is it critical that Jesus' own people, Israel, acknowledge him as God's Son?

Why does God allow us to choose whether or not to say yes to Jesus?

WEEK 39: READING 1

Leader Notes

The promise made to Abraham finds its ultimate fulfillment in the messianic king. The unexpected part is that he will be rejected by the establishment (Psalm 118:22) but still be king, nonetheless. That person is Jesus. He quotes the psalm in Luke 13:35. He is saying that he will return when the establishment, the leaders of his tribe, acknowledge him as their king. This is ironic because all his followers at this point are his own people, but the leaders of his people are rejecting him.

On this trip to Jerusalem for his final Passover things are getting very serious. Jesus and his followers have probably made this trip nearly every year of their lives since they were born. But for Jesus and the Twelve, this place is far more dangerous than anywhere else in their country. They are a threat to the powers in charge. They know this.

Jesus' predictions of his own death are upsetting. He says he will be resurrected, but his followers have no category in their minds for that. They are unable to process it. Jesus knows this but presses on.

WEEK 39

Reading 2

BIBLE STORY

Jesus seems to dishonor God by teaching how far down he stoops to show his love for us. But God does not worry about what we think of him.

Luke 15

Why does a father set aside his pride to welcome his lost son?

Why is the obedient son's anger dangerous and hard to get over?

How much does God love us? What should we do about it?

BIBLE CONVERSATION

Since the beginning, the Lord loves us and always seeks good for us.

Hosea 14

If God loves us, will he always protect us from our own foolish choices?

If God wants good things for us, why do we only seek out what we want?

In Hosea 14:9, why do the wise, intelligent, and just walk on the path of the Lord?

Leader Notes

The parable of the prodigal (lost) son who wastes his life is a picture of the lengths God is willing to go to redeem his children. God humiliates himself by not rejecting the bad son who represents the sinners and tax collectors Jesus is teaching. This is a surprise to the Pharisees and scribes whom Jesus is capturing in the character of the older son. The fact that Jesus takes on the limitations of human flesh to welcome his lost sons is a humiliation for the God of all creation.

Hosea reminds Israel where their degradation has brought them and assures them that God wants good things for them. God is compassionate and deeply loves his people. We forget that so easily when things don't go the way we want. We think God should make life accommodate all our lusts and petty jealousies. We are foolish creatures, like two-year-olds pitching a fit in a store about a toy our parent will not buy for us.

WEEK 39

Reading 3

BIBLE STORY

Jesus teaches what will come in the days ahead and on the final day.

Luke 17:11–37

Why is the kingdom of God here when Jesus is here (Luke 17:21)?

If Jesus now lives in us, how is the kingdom of God here?

When Jesus returns, how will the kingdom of God be here even more so?

BIBLE CONVERSATION

Sometimes in human history the Lord acts so that no one misses what is going on.

Isaiah 29:5–8

What things in life make us wish for the day when the Lord returns suddenly, in an instant?

Why is injustice and evil a reminder that the Lord is not yet finished?

Why is it good to be on God's side even when things are not going well?

WEEK 39: READING 3

Leader Notes

Jesus' teaching about the kingdom of God breaks a lot of preconceived notions for his listeners. They ask in Luke 17:20 when the kingdom will come and Jesus essentially says, "You are looking at it." Yes, all things will be made right, all accounts settled at some point in history. But, when God takes on flesh, he is here. Wherever he is, there is the kingdom. So, if he dwells in his people—us—the kingdom is there.

The Lord living in his people is the kingdom of God spreading its influence all over the earth and in every generation. In the kingdom to come, God's presence will dwell among us more directly than now. Jesus says not to spend our time trying to guess which event signals his return, but rather to live each day like he is returning this day.

WEEK 40

Reading 1

BIBLE STORY

Jesus does one last miracle to open the disciples' eyes to his coming death and resurrection.

John 11:1–7, 20–57

Why do Martha, Mary, and the mourners all say to Jesus, "If only you would have been here, he would not have died?"

Why is it important that the writer John notices how Lazarus is trapped by his burial clothes, but soon after Jesus is not trapped by his burial clothes?

When everyone sees Lazarus alive, why do lots of people believe in Jesus, but a few decide that he must die?

BIBLE CONVERSATION

The power that the disciples are seeing with their eyes has always existed.

Isaiah 40:21–26

How great is the God who gives life, brings ruin, and creates the stars at night?

How hard would it be to believe that the person you just had dinner with is the God in Isaiah 40?

WEEK 40: READING 1

Leader Notes

Jesus and the disciples are avoiding the growing political danger in Jerusalem by staying in the desert where John used to baptize. But Passover is coming, and now they receive news that Lazarus is ill. Jesus waits, lets the pressure build, then finally starts for Jerusalem.

The disciples have seen him raise someone who just died, but now Lazarus is in the tomb four days. His flesh is rotting, his spirit is long gone. Their understanding of who Jesus is is being stretched one last time before the big stretch, when Jesus himself is dead.

John is focused on the grave clothes of Lazarus; how Lazarus is made alive and must be freed from his wrappings. Later he will focus on Jesus' abandoned grave wrappings. Why and how is the resurrection of Jesus different than the resurrection of Lazarus?

When Jesus raises Lazarus near Jerusalem many influential Jewish leaders see it. Many important people believe, and other important people are suddenly threatened in a new profound way. Those threatened decide that Jesus will cause them to lose power and influence. He must die.

WEEK 40

Reading 2

BIBLE STORY

After raising Lazarus, Jesus enters the great city as its king.

Luke 19:28–48

Why does Jesus now allow the crowds to call him king, when before, he left when they did it (John 6:15)?

Why would they think he is a king?

Why can we trust him more than anyone else to be our king?

BIBLE CONVERSATION

Jesus weeps over what God wants to do for Israel, but the political and religious leadership will not have it.

Isaiah 40:27–31

Why is waiting on the Lord such a big deal in the Bible?

What does it mean to wait on him?

What do we learn from Jesus about waiting on the Lord?

WEEK 40: READING 2

Leader Notes

The crowds are welcoming Jesus to the city at Passover like the priests are supposed to welcome the king to the temple. There has not been a king over Israel for a long time. The Romans are in charge. Herod is a king but not Jewish, not theirs, and they hate him. Jesus now presents himself to the Jewish nation as their king. Many people want him, but the rulers do not. He brings no army to defeat the Romans. His followers will hold him as king in their hearts after the resurrection. They will carry their allegiance throughout all the world.

Jesus is God's gift to the nation. He is not the gift they think they want. Isaiah long ago addressed Israel's complaint that the Lord does not give them what they want. Jesus is now the gift, and the leadership balks.

WEEK 40

Reading 3

BIBLE STORY

In the city that week, Jesus helps his disciples focus on the chaos coming and the days beyond.

Matthew 24:1–35

Why is it important that the questions asked of Jesus all center around the temple in Jerusalem?

Why does Jesus tell them not to believe any signs except seeing the Lord himself?

How does looking forward to the Lord's return affect the way we live every day? Today?

BIBLE CONVERSATION

In the heavenly places we will be struck with wonder at all these things.

Revelation 19:6–10

Why is God inviting us to the best party ever?

Who is the Lamb?

What is the occasion?

WEEK 40: READING 3

Leader Notes

There are several ways that people approach the interpretation of Matthew 24. The most straightforward is to pay attention to where Jesus and the disciples are, and the questions being answered. The location and conversation are about the temple. The Mount of Olives overlooks the temple. There will be many troubles for that central place in Israel. The return of the Messiah is tied to the land of Israel and the Jewish people.

The temple and Jesus the Messiah are at the center of how God fulfills his original promise to Abraham. It completely affects all humanity but is centered where it started.

In the Revelation scene, the Lamb is Jesus, and the wedding banquet reunites Jesus with his people. It is the fulfillment of everything hoped for, the most glorious day ever.

WEEK 41

Reading 1

BIBLE STORY

Jesus' public ministry is tireless. His entry into Jerusalem attracts a lot of attention. But his innermost heart is with his disciples.

John 13

Why does Jesus wash Judas's feet along with everyone else's?

Why is it important to know about Passover to understand what is going on here?

Why and how is Peter's denial going to be different than Judas's betrayal?

BIBLE CONVERSATION

Knowing that terrible things are ahead, Jesus acts resolutely as the servant of God.

Isaiah 42:1–4

Why is Isaiah talking about Jesus hundreds of years before?

How is Jesus still establishing justice on the earth through our lives?

How will we all finally live by his justice?

WEEK 41: READING 1

Leader Notes

All the disciples and Jesus have been coming to Jerusalem to celebrate Passover almost every year their whole lives. Their people have been doing this since the time of Moses, a millennium and a half ago. They all know how to do this. So, the changes that Jesus brings really stand out to them.

Judas's betrayal and Peter's denial are being compared by all the Gospel writers. What is the difference? Why is one condemned and the other forgiven? These questions grow as the story deepens. They are not simple or easy to answer.

Isaiah moves us into the first of what are called the servant songs describing this one who will come. What kind of king is Jesus?

WEEK 41

Reading 2

BIBLE STORY

After Judas leaves their Passover supper, Jesus continues sharing many intimate things with the disciples.

John 14:1-7, 12-19; 16:5-16

Why is it so good to know that we have a place in the house of our Heavenly Father?

Why is the Helper, the Holy Spirit, so important for living today?

Why is Jesus telling his followers all of this as the last things before he dies?

BIBLE CONVERSATION

Jesus comes to seek and save the lost, as the prophets foretell.

Isaiah 49:5-7, 14-16

Why is this servant of the Lord going to bring Israel back to the Lord?

Why is this servant of the Lord going to be a light for all the people of the earth?

Who is this servant? Can we know him?

WEEK 41: READING 2

Leader Notes

Jesus leads the Twelve into Jerusalem. It is very dangerous for them. They must stay hidden when they are not out with the crowds. He now tells his close disciples that he is leaving; they are desperately afraid of being abandoned. They are trapped in the city. He has been telling them, but we humans often cannot hear things we are not ready for.

Jesus is stretching them farther than they are ready. They will never be ready for this. But he wants them to have heard this so that when the trauma of what is about to happen eases, they will remember. The Holy Spirit will help them remember. The Holy Spirit in Jesus' followers will be the presence of God in the world, just like Jesus is the presence of God in the world while he is here.

Isaiah, in his servant songs, long before Jesus, expands the reach of this servant beyond even Israel to the nations. This will be hard for Israel to accept because they got in so much trouble for acting like the nations around them. They know to stay away from the nations that worship idols and act immorally.

WEEK 41

Reading 3

BIBLE STORY

At the final Passover with his disciples, Jesus ties the matzo and the cup of redemption to his own body and blood. The sacrifice lamb that takes away the sins of the world will be sacrificed once and for all.

Luke 22:14–38

Why is Jesus called the "Passover sacrifice lamb" (John 1:29)?

Why is the Passover celebration so central to who Israel is?

Why do we take this part of the Passover, the Lord's Supper, as part of following Jesus?

BIBLE CONVERSATION

Centuries before, the Lord reveals that his peace, joy, and salvation are coming through his amazing servant.

Isaiah 52:7–10

How important is having peace and joy?

Why are peace and joy better than anything we own or get to do?

How can we be part of God's peace, joy, and salvation?

WEEK 41: READING 3

Leader Notes

Jesus' role as the sacrifice lamb was already located in the Passover. Just as God's judgment passed over the Israelites long ago in Egypt because they painted the blood of the lamb on their door lintels, so now Jesus' blood protects from the judgment of God. Just as God redeemed his people from slavery to the Egyptians, so now he redeems a people from slavery to sin. There is no more central piece of connection between Jesus and his people. The early mostly gentile churches apparently celebrate the Passover (1 Corinthians 5:6–8; Acts 20:6). Jewish followers of Jesus today celebrate the Passover and share that with many gentile churches as well. God has changed the world forever with his Passover Lamb.

This world change is seen long before Jesus walks in this world as one of us. The deep change comes through him and affects everyone.

WEEK 42

Reading 1

BIBLE STORY

After Jesus and his disciples finish the Passover supper, they go out into the night.

Luke 22:39–65

What is Jesus tempted to do?

Why does Jesus tell his disciple to put away the sword he told them to keep earlier at dinner?

What is the difference between Judas's betrayal and Peter's denial?

BIBLE CONVERSATION

Isaiah foretells the ugly reality of man rejecting God.

Isaiah 52:13–15

How can a victorious coming king suffer and be disfigured?

What is God's surprising, coming secret?

WEEK 42: READING 1

Leader Notes

The amount of danger Jesus and the disciples are in is reflected in the fact that they are hiding. Jesus, knowing their secret location has been compromised is tempted to get his disciples out of danger. It is deeper, though. He is tempted as a human, not to endure the pain and misery of all human sin and guilt dying on a Roman cross. He is asking the Father to take this away.

Peter, another Gospel tells us, is the disciple who swings his sword at an official person. He commits a crime to protect Jesus. Luke, in this chapter, weaves the theme of swords all the way through from the supper to Jesus final statement in the garden. There is no clear answer to why Jesus tells them to take a sword but then does not let them use it. We have to work on that our whole life; when is it okay to defend ourselves and when do we let our fate be with the Lord?

There is no clear answer about Judas and Peter, but one is condemned and the other redeemed. It forces us to engage this story deeply and personally all our life.

Isaiah begins his final servant song about the coming king, victorious but suffering. It will not be clear or understood until it happens, a mystery.

WEEK 42

Reading 2

BIBLE STORY

For healing, loving, and speaking truth, Jesus endures vicious beatings and humiliation. The powerful of humanity, Jews and gentiles, sentence Jesus to die a horrible death.

Luke 22:66—23:25

Why do all the officials bother to have a trial when they already know what they are going to do?

If Pilate really cares about justice, as he pretends, what should he do?

Who is really in control when this is happening (John 19:10–11)?

BIBLE CONVERSATION

The deep irony of a righteous servant suffering is foretold centuries before. Our sorrow is deeper when we see that our own sin brings this to pass.

Isaiah 53:1–6

How can what seems like losing be God's solution to our problems?

What are transgressions and iniquities?

Why is God so serious about all this?

WEEK 42: READING 2

Leader Notes

The Gospels each give an accounting for the trial of Jesus. The various political groups are trying to get each other to take responsibility for the sham proceeding going on in the night. In the end Pilate does not want riots that Caesar will hear about, so he agrees, and Jesus is to be crucified as a common rebel. Pilate is willing to deal out the harshest death possible just for convenience. He does not hate Jesus like the religious leaders, he just does not care. They are all culpable.

Theologically, this is the collective voice of all humankind rejecting God. All of humanity is in on this because we all sin. He bears our transgressions and iniquities. All the suffering we endure or cause lands on this righteous servant. It is a hopeless hypocrisy if we say, "I would have tried to save him," or "I would not have participated in this."

WEEK 42

Reading 3

BIBLE STORY

In a spectacle horrifying to behold, the Lamb of God takes away the sin of all who will receive this gift.

Luke 23:26–56

Why is Jesus, a young construction worker, unable to carry the one-hundred-pound crossbeam?

Why does the thief in verses 40–43 enter paradise with Jesus?

Why is Jesus able to leave his body when his mission is finished (Luke 23:46)?

BIBLE CONVERSATION

Long foretold by the prophets, the reality comes to pass in the history of humankind.

Isaiah 53:7–9

How does the death of Jesus seem like the fulfillment of this prophecy from hundreds of years before?

Why is the transgression in verse 8 so important and expensive?

What is the cost of our transgression?

Leader Notes

All four Gospels record this event from their perspective and purpose. The Gospels are eyewitness accounts, but not like newspapers claiming to be "just the facts." They are each written to a different audience for a different reason. John's Gospel says that he "writes that you might believe" (John 20:31). Jesus' death and resurrection is the historical touchpoint that the truth of the Gospels turn on.

Roman crucifixion is the most horrifying, humiliating execution they can devise for the purpose of intimidating local populations they control. It is reserved for criminals, slaves, and foreigners. Jesus is probably beaten so badly during the trial that he is in shock and has already lost so much blood that he may not survive even without crucifixion. The execution soldiers are likely mostly locals—not Jewish—that harbor longstanding resentment against Jewish people. Their job is to leave enough life in the person being executed to be crucified before they die.

The picture of the lamb led to slaughter is an ancient part of the Passover that everyone understands. The difficulty for most is to tie that picture with the victorious Messiah King described elsewhere in Isaiah and the other prophets.

WEEK 43

Reading 1

BIBLE STORY

The death of Jesus is not the end of the story.

Luke 24:1–32

Why is it hard for the women and apostles to remember and believe that Jesus will rise from the dead?

Why does Peter run to the tomb to see for himself?

Why can the disciples on the road to Emmaus not recognize that they are talking to Jesus?

BIBLE CONVERSATION

Isaiah foretells the resurrection of the Messiah a long time before.

Isaiah 53:10–12

In verse 10, who are Jesus' "offspring?"

What does that mean for us?

Why does dying for our sins make Jesus the King of everyone and everything (Isaiah 53:12)?

WEEK 43: READING 1

Leader Notes

The crucifixion of Jesus has the effect intended by the Romans: shock, horror, and intimidation. For Jesus' followers, all the hopes of him being their king have blown away in this hurricane of horrid events. His followers and family are neither forgetful nor faithless; they are human. They have been traumatized, by design. The world system has officially rejected God.

Jesus begins the appearances in his resurrected body. He teaches and explains before they recognize him. He gives them bread. He disappears. There will be much more.

Isaiah makes clear that the death of the servant of the Lord for the transgressions of his people is not the end. The servant wins the victory. To see one's offspring is to have a future; for him, death is not the end. We who are in Jesus are his children, his offspring.

WEEK 43

Reading 2

BIBLE STORY

After the resurrection of Jesus, he appears to his followers and prepares them to be his sent-out ones.

Luke 24:33–53

How do they know that Jesus is not a ghost?

Why is it important that all the Scripture speaks of all the things they have seen?

What does it mean that they will be clothed with power from on high?

BIBLE CONVERSATION

Resurrection from the dead is centered on trust in the giver of life.

Psalm 16:5–11

How has the Lord made our heritage beautiful?

How does the Lord counsel us?

Why do the apostles Peter and Paul later use verses 10 and 11 to show the resurrection of Jesus in Acts 2:25–28 and 13:35?

Leader Notes

Jesus' appearances after the resurrection are important. The disciples, now apostles, eventually lose their lives because of the gospel. That lends huge credibility to their eyewitness testimony of seeing the resurrected Jesus. Eyewitnesses do not willingly die for things they do not believe really happened.

Jesus eats with them, and they can touch his wounds and flesh. Yes, it really is him! He teaches from the Scriptures. He gives at Luke 24:44 his divisions of the Scripture: the Law, the Prophets, and the Psalms. Psalms is the first book of the final section of the Hebrew Bible, also called the Writings. The order of the books is different than the Greek translation of the Old Testament and is important for understanding the messianic nature of the Hebrew Bible.

WEEK 43

Reading 3

BIBLE STORY

John tells the resurrection story from his perspective as an eyewitness.

John 20

As the writer John remembers Lazarus struggling in his death linens, what does he do when he sees Jesus' death linens in the tomb (John 20:5–8)?

What does Mary have in common with the fellows on the road to Emmaus in Luke's Gospel (John 20:14)?

Do you think Thomas sticks his finger into the place where the spear pierced Jesus?

BIBLE CONVERSATION

The idea of three days is not new to the Gospels. The disciples are experiencing God's long-developing realities and moving closer to him.

Hosea 6:1–3

What does the resurrection of Jesus have to do with us who believe? Is it good?

Can we make God go away if we don't believe in him or don't like him?

WEEK 43: READING 3

Leader Notes

John gives us his personal eyewitness account of the resurrection likely after the other three Gospels are written. He emphasizes having seen Lazarus struggling in his death linens and then in the empty tomb that Jesus has come right up through his death linens. Jesus' resurrection is quite different. Lazarus is going to experience death again. Jesus' body is an eternal resurrection body—the same now and forever—that is not bound by doors and walls. He is more solid than the disciples but can appear and disappear at will.

John tells us that he believes before he sees the resurrected Jesus. He believes when he sees the linens. Everyone else seems to have to see Jesus before they believe. John tells us he writes these things so that we too might believe before we lay our eyes on Jesus.

WEEK 44

Reading 1

BIBLE STORY

John in his own Gospel is always with his friend Peter. John sees Peter restored to Jesus after his earlier denial.

John 21

What does the catch of fish, the fire, and the breakfast show us about the risen Jesus?

Why does Jesus ask Peter three times if he loves him?

Why do we know many more things happened that we will hear about later?

BIBLE CONVERSATION

The Lord is always bringing us back to himself after we do wrong. He feels deeply about us.

Isaiah 54:1–8

Why is the wife in this prophetic story like Peter hearing the three questions?

Why is this like all of us who come to be reconciled with the Lord?

WEEK 44: READING 1

Leader Notes

Every time the writer John mentions himself in his own Gospel account—*"the disciple whom Jesus loved"*—he is with Peter. He is at the tomb, the fishing boat, and the interview between Peter and Jesus. He is keen to show us that he also is a disciple of Jesus but quite a different kind than bold, brash Peter.

The three times asking Peter "Do you love me?" is a restoration of the three denials of Peter at Jesus' trial. This sets Peter in clear contrast to Judas Iscariot, who is condemned and not restored. We can ask, "What if he never killed himself and came back?" but that is speculation the Gospel does not entertain, and we must live with it, trying to understand and being warned about our own unbelief.

Isaiah's picture of the cast-out wife who is reconciled is a picture of Israel and the Babylonian exile in its first instance. But it serves as a stirring look at God being reconciled with whomever of us will come to him as he reaches out to our sad, broken world.

WEEK 44

Reading 2

BIBLE STORY

Luke begins his ongoing story of Jesus' followers with Jesus being taken into heaven. What will they do now?

Acts 1

What do we learn from the first verses of Luke's two-volume set of books, Luke 1:1–4 and Acts 1:1–3?

Why is Jesus' answer "not yet" to the disciple's good question about restoring the kingdom to Israel?

How important do you think Jesus' mother and brothers (Acts 1:14) are to the early church in Jerusalem?

BIBLE CONVERSATION

The early believers do not yet realize it, but they are entering a new age that God prepared for his people.

Isaiah 54:9–10

How has this promise to Israel also been fulfilled for all who follow Israel's Messiah Jesus?

Why is it wonderful and amazing that God's love will not depart from us?

Leader Notes

Luke wrote the Gospel of Luke and the book of Acts. They are both about the same size, each big enough to fill a standard scroll of that day. Luke tells us he gathered eyewitness reports from others. He is an eyewitness and traveling companion late in the story, joining with the traveling party of Paul at times, beginning in chapter 16 of Acts. The story of Jesus' ascension into heaven is told at the end of his Gospel and again at the beginning of Acts. It links the stories together.

Jesus' mother is obviously a source for the Gospels, especially the birth and childhood stories that are only in Matthew and Luke. Jesus' brothers James (Jacob) and Jude (Judah) both write a letter that is in the New Testament. James is the head of the Jerusalem church after James the brother of John is murdered by Herod. Jesus' physical relatives are, no doubt, an important touchpoint for the early church as it struggles for survival.

Peter and the others are now apostles, "sent out ones," where in the Gospels they are disciples, "followers." Luke does refer to them as apostles late in his Gospel. They gather up and organize, waiting to be empowered for their mission.

WEEK 44

Reading 3

BIBLE STORY

When Jesus ascends into the heavens, the Holy Spirit comes upon the believers, as Jesus promises. Peter, in the power of the Holy Spirit, boldly preaches the gospel from the Scriptures.

Acts 2

Why does the Holy Spirit have this band of Jesus people speak in different languages?

Why is it important that the Scriptures speak about Jesus before he shows up?

What parts of getting saved and following Jesus have changed since that day of Pentecost?

BIBLE CONVERSATION

The choice is clear; men and women need to say yes to God.

Isaiah 55:1-5

Why do most things *we* plan look like what *we* imagine?

Why do things planned by God—like Pentecost in Acts 2—look so different than we expect?

Leader Notes

When Jesus walks among us, he is the temple. He is the place God chooses to dwell on earth. When he goes back into the heavens to rule as our king, he sends the Holy Spirit to make his people the temple. We are the place God chooses to dwell on earth.

The purpose of the foreign tongues on the celebration of Pentecost is so that the Jewish people, gathered from all over the known world, know that God is present in his Jesus-following people. Everyone in this story is Jewish. They know languages in common. Peter probably speaks to them in Aramaic. But the tongues they hear from the believers are in their birth languages.

God knows us. He knows where we are from. He knows the language in which we think and dream. He wants us to know his son Jesus, our Messiah in the deepest places of our mind and soul.

Peter brings it home with a message that expounds the Scripture—there is not yet a New Testament. It is a Jewish message that resonates, and thousands respond to this fisherman from Galilee who has recently denied his Lord.

The description of the embryonic church in Jerusalem is founded on principles—the apostle's teaching (what becomes our New Testament), fellowship, the Lord's Supper, and prayer—that are still the core of who we are and what we do.

WEEK 45

Reading 1

BIBLE STORY

When the Holy Spirit comes upon the timid and confused disciples, they begin to act as bold apostles.

Acts 3

What changes in the lame man's life?

When a crowd gathers what does Peter do? Why?

Why is Peter so different now than when Jesus was here?

BIBLE CONVERSATION

A clear line is drawn; will we trust Jesus or not?

Isaiah 55:6–13

What does God want for us? How good is it?

Why is God able to bring things that are good and new?

If mountains sing and trees clap their hands, what should we be doing to praise God?

WEEK 45: READING 1

Leader Notes

Peter and John work together here, as in John's Gospel. Luke shows Peter doing the same things Jesus is tried and executed for. Peter boldly proclaims the gospel. His message about Jesus being the Jewish Messiah is this time based in the law of Moses, whereas in the previous chapter it was based in the Prophets and Psalms. The New Testament understands Jesus as a clear fulfillment of the Old Testament from the promise of Abraham to the Law of Moses, to David's throne that the Messiah will sit upon. The sermons in the book of Acts are a great way to understand the gospel message of the early church. It should be the same message in our church.

WEEK 45

Reading 2

BIBLE STORY

When the apostles begin to proclaim the gospel in Jerusalem, the same people who opposed Jesus rise up against them.

Acts 4

As good citizens, when are we obligated to disobey the authorities?

Why is that a dangerous thing to do? What cost might we pay?

Why is it important to keep praying for others standing for the gospel in dangerous places?

BIBLE CONVERSATION

God always seeks the hearts of his people.

Isaiah 59:1–3, 15b–20

What do we all have in common when we stand before God?

Why do we have patience with people who choose to disobey God?

WEEK 45: READING 2
Leader Notes

Peter speaks after being arrested by the temple authorities. The temple complex is the biggest economic engine in the country. Many people make their living, and some their fortunes, from it. People whose livelihoods are threatened can be dangerous. This is the same storm brewing as happened to Jesus. The authorities think they defeated Jesus, but these Galilean fishermen are not going home to Galilee. They remain in the city and are causing trouble.

The reason Peter and John are released is because they are uneducated, and the practice is to warn people—especially people who may not know better—before punishing them. This is the warning, and we will see them punished later for continuing to preach the gospel of Jesus, the risen Jewish Messiah.

The topic of civil disobedience is front and center here. We must think hard about if and when to disobey laws and authorities. God promises to be with us but may or may not deliver us from punishment. Sometimes Jesus and his followers defy the authorities. More often they hide. The church is later scattered by persecution. That is mostly how the gospel spread, by people running away from trouble. This is not a simple decision most times, and we need to be in close contact with the Lord and one another. We also need to think carefully about how we teach our children and lead by example.

WEEK 45

Reading 3

BIBLE STORY

After Peter's testimony before the High Priest, the Holy Spirit reinforces the seriousness of serving God with a whole heart.

Acts 5

Why is telling the truth so important in the community of Jesus followers?

How could the apostles rejoice at being badly beaten with whips (Acts 5:40–42)?

How is the community of Jesus becoming strong?

BIBLE CONVERSATION

The apostles become irrepressible. God has that effect on those who trust him.

Isaiah 60:1–3

What are some ways the Lord brings light into our dark world?

How do Jesus followers bring light?

WEEK 45: READING 3

Leader Notes

What becomes clear in the Ananias story is that they brought the money saying it was all the money. As Peter makes clear to Sapphira, they can do whatever they want except lie to receive more credit than they deserve. Persecution strengthens and grows the church, but corruption causes it to begin rotting. This is a portent of things to come. Many over the centuries will have to answer to God for the corruption in his church.

The Lord gets them out of jail miraculously so they can continue to preach. Gamaliel the Pharisee is Paul's teacher. He defends the believers here from the same death sentence as Jesus. But this time they are punished. Flogging is a horrible, damaging punishment. But they, especially Peter, who denied Jesus, now consider it a privilege to suffer for Jesus.

WEEK 46

Reading 1

BIBLE STORY

After a bold beginning, the young church faces some practical problems and finds another bold witness.

Acts 6:1—7:8; 7:51—8:1a

Why is it important that the whole group agrees when doing big new things (Acts 6:5)?

If Stephen is speaking wisdom by the Spirit (Acts 6:10), why does he end up dying?

Why does God allow the gospel to be spread by the trouble that comes to the new church (Acts 8:1)?

BIBLE CONVERSATION

Stephen is simply following in the footsteps of Jesus.

Isaiah 61:1–3

Why do we often see God's truth more clearly in hard times than good?

How do we know that God loves us even when things are difficult?

WEEK 46: READING 1

Leader Notes

All the characters in the story are Jewish. The Hellenists are Jewish followers of Jesus whose first language is Greek. This likely indicates that they were born in a Jewish community outside the land of Israel but now live in Jerusalem. This community is often more zealous for Judaism than home-born Israelites who speak Hebrew or Aramaic as their mother tongue. All or most of the newly appointed deacons appear to be Hellenists.

Stephen's unbelieving fellow Hellenists are afraid of being seen in a bad light by the Sanhedrin, so they are not receptive to this new message of the risen Jewish Messiah. The believing Hellenists are an important part of the new church. The original dispute about feeding widows is portrayed as a growing pain that is resolved by community consent. Widows are particularly vulnerable in that world. Girls are often married off by arrangement in their early teens to older men who can afford to support a family. Most often the older man dies first, leaving a younger wife with no means of support. There are many widows and orphans.

Stephen is killed because of his faith, and the "magical" time of the new church is over. Trouble breaks out for everyone, and we are introduced to Saul, a young man perhaps in his mid-twenties, who will become another major character in the New Testament story.

WEEK 46

Reading 2

BIBLE STORY

After the death of Stephen, persecution creates growth in the fledgling church.

Acts 8:1b–25

Why is there hostility between the Jewish people and the Samaritans?

If we had to move to a new town because we follow Jesus, why would that be hard?

If we had to move to a new place among strangers, would we want to talk to them about Jesus? Why?

BIBLE CONVERSATION

What God is preparing will be worth far more than all the difficulty of sharing his truth with an unwilling world.

Isaiah 65:17–25

Why will God make a new heavens and new earth like he says here and again in Revelation 21:1?

If everything today does not work out, why can I be confident that God loves me?

WEEK 46: READING 2

Leader Notes

The Gospels are full of stories about Samaritans and how much hostility is between them and the Jewish people. Samaritans are mostly people who are from the other tribes of Israel that fell out of favor because they intermarried with foreigners and did not worship in Jerusalem. Jesus has a very instructive conversation with the woman at the well about this in John 4.

The church seems to grow when there is pressure on it. Peter is called to Samaria and the Holy Spirit is given to the Samaritans. This is probably a surprise that God cares about them, but the gospel is received, and God treats them as equals with the believers from Jerusalem.

WEEK 46

Reading 3

BIBLE STORY

The gospel is taken into Samaria, as Jesus said. God then prepares an unlikely candidate to take the gospel to the gentiles.

Acts 9:1–31

Why is Saul an unlikely person for the Lord to pick for his service?

Why is everyone in the Jerusalem church afraid of Saul (Acts 9:26)?

Who will you be surprised to see become a follower of Jesus?

BIBLE CONVERSATION

Regardless of our religious background or birth, God is looking at our heart.

Isaiah 66:1–2

Why are eighth-brother David and carpenter's-son Jesus such a surprise to everyone as kings of Israel?

Why is it too easy for God to surprise us?

Why is it hard for us to understand everything God tells us?

WEEK 46: READING 3

Leader Notes

Saul seems a very unlikely choice for the church, since he is trying to destroy it. God knows what he is looking for. It is no coincidence that there is peace for the church when Saul starts following Jesus (Acts 9:31). The believers quickly find out that Saul is a stronger force for the Lord than he was against. Those around him will often have to protect him from the reaction to his evangelizing.

In Isaiah's final chapter, he reminds us why God is always surprising us. He does not have to deceive us. But rather we deceive ourselves by looking at temples, physical strength, physical beauty, and beautiful words. We tend to focus on all the wrong things. As we learn to look at people's hearts, we are less surprised by what God does.

WEEK 47

Reading 1

BIBLE STORY

After Saul the persecutor meets Jesus, Peter introduces the gospel to the gentiles as he had to the Jews and Samaritans.

Acts 10

For Peter, why is eating unclean food like taking the gospel to gentiles?

What group of people do you always feel uncomfortable around? Why?

Why does God ask us to do good things that are uncomfortable?

BIBLE CONVERSATION

Because of troubles in the past, no self-respecting Jewish person imagines that God will bring the gentiles to himself, but there is a time for everything.

Ecclesiastes 3:1–11

Why do we pick fruit when it is ripe?

How do we know when it is time for something new?

What does Ecclesiastes 3:11 mean that everything is beautiful in its time?

WEEK 47: READING 1

Leader Notes

Bringing the gospel to the whole world is a big milestone in God's plan. In ancient times Israel is severely punished for living like the gentiles around them. They learn their lesson and do not wish to repeat it. Now God is asking Peter to enter that forbidden world.

Understanding something and overcoming our feelings about it can be two extremely different things. This is more than a theoretical exercise; it is a person with a name.

Acts 10:23–25 is more significant than it initially appears; Peter invites gentiles into his house and then goes into the house of a gentile. The thought of that for Peter is perhaps the emotional equivalent of entering a basement full of snakes and spiders. Now he understands differently, but how does he feel? Regardless of how he feels, he does it. He is obedient, and God blesses him. The Holy Spirit is poured out on gentiles, which means God loves them the same as Jewish people; unthinkable!

The Bible story encompasses all of human life and experience. Ecclesiastes captures that in this beautiful section.

WEEK 47

Reading 2

BIBLE STORY

A decade or so after Jesus' final Passover with his disciples, Saul is working in the big church at Antioch in Syria. In Jerusalem at Passover, a new Herod brings pressure on Jesus' people again.

Acts 12:1–24

Why does Peter seem unafraid now, unlike when he denied Jesus at Passover in Jerusalem all those years ago?

Why does Peter not enter the house, but go somewhere safer after the miraculous escape (Acts 12:17)? Is he now afraid or acting wisely?

Why do we have to let God carry out justice and not do it ourselves?

BIBLE CONVERSATION

Herod is not a god, and the church does not grow because of any human strength or cleverness.

Jeremiah 9:23–24

Why does God care so much about what we are like in our mind and heart?

WEEK 47: READING 2

Leader Notes

Herod is a different-but-related person to the Herod at Jesus' trial. He is different again, but related, to the Herod at Jesus' birth. The Herods rule over the Jewish people but are hated by them. They are of part-Jewish lineage and desperately want to be respected by them. They take any opportunity to ingratiate themselves with the Jewish leadership. This Herod murders the apostle John's brother James and arrests Peter at Passover. This surely seems to Peter to be setting him up to redeem himself for denying the Lord at Passover a decade or so ago. He is perhaps thinking that he will die at Passover too.

But Peter is a servant of Jesus, not a grandstander looking out for his own reputation. When the angel takes him out of prison, he lets the believers know that God is afoot. Peter does not stay there. He knows the authorities will come there first looking for him. He takes that release from prison to mean that he has more work to do before he dies; so, he gets on to it.

Jeremiah assures us, long before Peter's time, that the Lord will deal with people like Herod. Those people love only themselves and only ever pretend to be good or do right.

WEEK 47

Reading 3

BIBLE STORY

After Peter is released from prison in Jerusalem by an angel, Saul and Barnabas are set apart to carry the gospel out from Antioch in Syria.

Acts 13

Why do Saul and Barnabas take the gospel message to the synagogue wherever they go?

How do they come to sharing the message with gentiles?

How does God teach us by making us go out and try new things?

BIBLE CONVERSATION

Despite opposition, the disciples are filled with joy because they know whom they are serving.

Jeremiah 17:5–11

Why can we be patient with people who don't like us?

Who will give us that patience?

WEEK 47: READING 3

Leader Notes

Saul and Barnabas sail to Cyprus and go across the island teaching in synagogues. Jesus barely ever left the land of Israel, and this message was first and foremost for the Jewish people. Peter had superintended the pouring out of the Holy Spirit on Cornelius the gentile centurion, but there was no mission to the gentiles.

It is the magician on Cyprus that seems to clarify things for Saul. At verse 9 in Saul's meeting with a gentile official, Luke starts calling him Paul. The result of this meeting is that this official becomes a follower of Jesus. He is a gentile with no apparent connection to the synagogue. Saul, now Paul, apparently has a new strategy to go to the marketplace after the synagogue when they sail across to what is modern-day Turkey.

It is possible that John Mark leaves because of that new idea. He, perhaps, feels like how Peter felt. He does not go back to Antioch, but rather Jerusalem, where the mother-church and his mother are. He may well have stirred up Pharisee-tradition believers there to oppose Paul later in an incident recorded in Acts and Galatians.

This inside-the-church opposition is brewing while Paul and Barnabas are facing opposition outside the new churches they are planting. The great result is that there are new groups of Jewish and gentile believers in every town where they go.

WEEK 48

Reading 1

BIBLE STORY

After Paul and Barnabas are thrown out of Pisidian Antioch they go to the next cities. They heal a man with unexpected results.

Acts 14

Why is it wise to avoid conflict whenever possible (Acts 14:5–7)?

Why do Paul and Barnabas come back to the cities where they were injured (Acts 14:21–23)?

What is the difference between doing what the Lord asks and being reckless to gain fame?

BIBLE CONVERSATION

Despite the opposition of established religion, God persists with his coming King.

Jeremiah 23:1–6

What is the difference being a responsible leader and taking advantage of people who trust us?

Why is God so willing to work with a small group—a remnant—that will do what he asks?

How will a righteous king be different from all the other leaders and politicians we ever hear about?

WEEK 48: READING 1

Leader Notes

We are so horrified by the violence of mobs reacting to Paul that we can miss the success in the story. In most of these places where the gospel is heard for the first time, a handful of people become followers of Jesus, which is the beginning of a new church. There is always a group of unknown people, disciples, who help the person under attack (usually Paul) get to safety.

Paul always starts in the synagogue, if there is one. When the gospel is presented, some Jewish people and some gentiles see that the Law, Prophets, and Writings—the Scripture they read—points to Jesus the Jewish Messiah. The leadership of this new church usually comes from the synagogue where they live by biblical morals and ethics and worship the God of Israel. Many of the new believers probably still attend the synagogue where their families and the center of their culture are.

The prophets speak about a remnant that God is willing to work with if the majority of people refuse to hear and obey him. A remnant is a minority who will do the right thing when it is unpopular or dangerous. These new churches are a remnant of the Jewish and gentile people called to obey God.

WEEK 48

Reading 2

BIBLE STORY

When Paul and Barnabas return from their first journey, another critical issue arises in the young church.

Acts 15:1–35

Why does God let the young church figure this out themselves without direct intervention?

How do the Spirit, Scripture, listening to others, and consensus bring the church to a good conclusion?

Why is it so amazing that the Spirit, Scripture, listening, and consensus moves the young church to a critical new idea?

BIBLE CONVERSATION

In Acts, accepting the gentiles is against the intuition of Jewish believers, just as accepting the exile to Babylon was hard centuries ago. But as always, it is about trusting God.

Jeremiah 29:4–11

Why are the Israelites supposed to settle in and live in the cities of Babylon where they are captive?

When is it hard to see that God wants good things for us?

Leader Notes

This is a critical milestone for the young church. The nation of Israel spent seventy years in captivity in Babylon because they got involved with the gods of their gentile neighbors. Part of serving the Lord, for them, is staying away from gentiles. Following the Jewish Messiah Jesus is taking them to places where their national, ethnic, and cultural identity is being tested.

James the brother of Jesus oversees the Jerusalem church. He leads the process of this council on the issue of gentiles in the church. The Lord does not intervene directly. He lets the church work it out by the influence of the Holy Spirit, the Scripture, the testimony of the apostles, the consensus of the group, and the leadership of James. James decides, articulates, and states the final decision.

In Jeremiah, Israel is asked to live under the dominion of the Babylonians. They are not necessarily nice people. This is against the instincts of the Israelites. They are asked to be strong and thrive in a difficult situation and trust that the Lord will help them. Many of their children come back to Jerusalem after seventy years and rebuild the city and temple. Many stay and form a significant Jewish community that lasts until the creation of the state of modern Israel in the twentieth century.

WEEK 48

Reading 3

BIBLE STORY

After the first major church council, Paul and Barnabas prepare for another missionary journey.

Acts 15:36—16:15

Why does the Lord let Paul and Barnabas break into two new teams?

Why is it important for Jewish Timothy to be circumcised to do ministry with Paul?

Why is it significant that the church at Philippi starts with a wealthy businesswoman?

BIBLE CONVERSATION

By choosing Timothy, who is Jewish and Greek, traveling with Luke the gentile physician, and centering the ministry at Philippi around a businesswoman named Lydia, Rabbi Paul understands how different this new covenant really is.

Jeremiah 31:31–34

Why does God let us figure out and work out so many new things?

The Lord wants us to know him; do you know him?

WEEK 48: READING 3

Leader Notes

John Mark's desertion and then the split-up of Paul and Barnabas probably has to do with taking the gospel to the gentiles directly in the marketplace. Everyone has strong personal feelings about it. When Paul is left for dead, Barnabas is with him, but John Mark is long gone. Paul does not trust John Mark. The Bible assesses no blame against Paul or Barnabas. Later in Paul's correspondence he has become friends again with John Mark. This John Mark is the one who writes the Gospel we call Mark.

The case of Timothy is important to understand Paul. He has likely written the letter we call Galatians already where he says in 3:28, "There is neither Jew nor Greek," and then in 5:2, "if you let yourself be circumcised, Messiah will be of no benefit to you." If the distinction between Jewish and gentile no longer exists in Messiah's community, why does he circumcise Timothy?

Given his action, his letter is not erasing all things Jewish, as some still wrongly teach. The passages in Galatians, in light of the Jerusalem council, mean that God does *not* like us better in any way because we are born Jewish, gentile, man, woman, slave, or free. Additionally, if we are born a gentile, converting to Judaism will not bring us closer to God or make him like us better. In fact, if we do that we are saying—by our action—that Jesus is not enough. We want to be someone other than who we were born.

Lydia in Philippi leads the founding household of the church there. The Bible recognizes differences between male and female role and responsibility, but no difference in value before God.

At the final Passover with the disciples Jesus says that the cup, which is now part of our communion, is Jeremiah's new covenant fulfilled.

WEEK 49

Reading 1

BIBLE STORY

As ministry for Paul, Silas, Timothy, and Luke opens up in gentile Philippi, brutal opposition brings new opportunities.

Acts 16:16–40

Why is it unjust and immoral to do what a mob wants just so things will quiet down?

Why are Paul and Silas singing and praising God in jail after being unjustly beaten?

Why do they wait until the situation is over to assert their legal rights as Roman citizens?

BIBLE CONVERSATION

While many opportunities are opening in the gentile world, Paul always starts with the synagogue because he knows that God is not yet finished with his people Israel.

Jeremiah 31:35–37

When will God stop caring about Israel?

Why is it good for all of us that God keeps his promises?

What is a promise we have because of Jesus?

WEEK 49: READING 1

Leader Notes

Paul remembers doing a miracle in the gentile marketplace on his first trip. The mob went from trying to worship him to stoning him. So, Paul ignores the spirit in the slave girl for many days. But he is provoked in his spirit and helps the girl be free. She probably becomes part of the new church in Philippi.

Once again, Paul's good deed gets him beaten by a mob, and this time thrown into prison. Paul and Silas could assert their legal rights as Roman citizens anytime but do not. They put themselves at God's mercy because the truth and credibility of the gospel is at stake.

When it becomes clear that Paul and Silas really mean what they say, by suffering for it, they address their legal rights. So, the new church is established with the jailer's household and Lydia's joining the other new believers.

Paul's patterns of ministry are founded on more than practical considerations. He knows that the Jewish Messiah is for the Jewish people, so he always starts with the Israelites wherever he goes. Philippi does not even have a synagogue, but Paul still finds the Jewish place of Sabbath prayers first thing there. This is where he meets Lydia.

WEEK 49

Reading 2

BIBLE STORY

After Paul is imprisoned in Philippi and causes a riot in Thessalonica, the believers send him on to Athens to wait for Timothy and Silas. He explains the gospel to the philosophers of Athens by starting with nature instead of the Bible story, which they know nothing about.

Acts 17:16–34

Why is it important to know about what other people think when we speak with them?

Why is it intimidating to speak with important people?

Why should we not be afraid to speak to people who seem more important than us if we have the opportunity?

BIBLE CONVERSATION

Even with all the outreach into the gentile world, God always intended to return the Jewish people to the land he gave them, and to put his Spirit in them.

Ezekiel 36:22–28

Where in the book of Acts is the Holy Spirit put into Jewish people in Israel?

What other people have received the Holy Spirit in this story?

Why is it so good to be part of God keeping his promises?

WEEK 49: READING 2

Leader Notes

Paul is very tuned in to what goes on around him. He begins his time in Athens, as usual, at the synagogue telling his people about their Messiah. He moves to the marketplace and ends up in the highest forum in the known world for discussing philosophy.

His gospel message in Athens begins where the Athenians are. They do not know the Bible, so Paul starts with their world, the idol to the unknown god and the created world all around. In the end there are believers from the synagogue and the Areopagus. God is working with open hearts.

We cannot all be Bible scholars and philosophers, but we can start where we are and listen to others. God works with what we bring and who we are. Most people come to the Lord because someone cares about them, rather than debating with them.

It is a joy to be part of God's promise to put his Spirit into whoever seeks him, starting with Israel and out to everyone.

WEEK 49

Reading 3

BIBLE STORY

After ministering in Athens, Corinth, and Ephesus, Paul makes his way back to Jerusalem, like Jesus, knowing that great opposition awaits him there.

Acts 20:6–38

Why doesn't Paul retire and relax now that he has worked for many years?

Why is it hard to say goodbye in a world without internet or smartphones?

What drives us? What kinds of things do you just have to finish, even if you are late to something else?

BIBLE CONVERSATION

Knowing that trouble is waiting for him in Jerusalem, Paul also knows that God means for Israel to be made spiritually alive, some day.

Ezekiel 37:1–14

Why does God make anyone more alive than they already are?

What does it mean to be born again?

WEEK 49: READING 3

Leader Notes

Paul is making his way back to Jerusalem after having Passover with the church at Philippi. He wanted to be in Jerusalem in time for Pentecost. He knows trouble is waiting for him there, and that God is drawing things to a close for him. He is running his race all the way through the finish line.

In the ancient world, there is little certainty of ever seeing someone again when they sail away in a boat. Days, months, and years go by without knowing about them. The churches are mourning the loss of Paul.

Ezekiel's vision is likely being fulfilled in our own time with the gathering of Jewish people from all over the world to Israel. The dry bones represent Israel awaiting the revival of God's spirit that is living in the gospel of Jesus the Messiah. There are more Jewish followers of Jesus now than ever before. The Spirit of the Lord is at work.

WEEK 50

Reading 1

BIBLE STORY

Despite repeated warnings from church leaders, Paul presses ahead to Jerusalem. His presence in the temple erupts into chaos.

Acts 21:30—22:29

What part of Paul's story makes his people get angry (Acts 22:21-22)?

Why is it hard for us that God loves people who have been bad to us?

How do we have courage to do the right thing on any given day?

BIBLE CONVERSATION

Paul puts himself in harm's way because he knows that he is serving Jesus. This Jesus is the Son of Man of whom Daniel speaks.

Daniel 7:1, 9-10, 13-14

Who is the Ancient of Days in Daniel's vision?

Why is it amazing that a human being—a son of man—is in the presence of the Ancient of Days?

What is amazing about this one human being? Who is he?

WEEK 50: READING 1

Leader Notes

Paul is taking the advice of the church leaders in Jerusalem in order to quell the rumors that he is blaspheming the main things they hold holy and dear, the Torah and the Temple. Paul knows that Jesus the Jewish Messiah, in fact, fulfills and gives those things their ultimate meaning. But people hear what they want to hear. Jewish people from everywhere gather for the biblical holidays—this is probably Pentecost (Shavuot) and the leaders from the places Paul has been evangelizing are there. They are not happy with what Paul has been doing in their communities all the way from Jerusalem to Athens.

After the riot starts Paul uses his Roman citizenship to change the situation, unlike in Philippi, where he waited and let himself be beaten for the sake of the gospel. This keeps him from immediate death and eventually takes him to Rome where he has opportunity to speak this gospel, perhaps, to Caesar himself.

Daniel, centuries before Jesus, sees a vision of a human standing in the presence of God. This is impossible; temporary, desire-driven flesh cannot stand before God. This is someone special. When Jesus comes, he calls himself the Son of Man, which is simply the Hebrew way of saying "human." But no one misses that Jesus is identifying himself with the human in Daniel's vision.

WEEK 50

Reading 2

BIBLE STORY

In Jerusalem, the Romans put Paul into protective custody because his fellow Israelites want to kill him. He is then permitted to address the Sanhedrin.

Acts 22:30—23:11

How much pressure is on Paul being under arrest and everyone wanting to kill him?

What does it mean that Paul is on trial because he has hope in the resurrection of the dead?

How many other people are safe at home praying for Paul? Why are there only a few like Paul?

BIBLE CONVERSATION

The Lord wants Paul to go to Rome. Paul is living by the Lord's timetable as are we all.

Daniel 12:1-4

Do we know how long our lives will be?

Who gives our life—however long—meaning?

Will you shine like the stars in the night for the Lord?

WEEK 50: READING 2

Leader Notes

Paul before the Sanhedrin uses his agile mind to get the Pharisees—from whom he came and with whom he mostly agrees—onto his side. The Lord stands by Paul to encourage him and tell him the big picture. It is a comforting picture that the Lord stands beside us instead of facing us. He is with us and looking ahead with us where we are going.

WEEK 50

Reading 3

BIBLE STORY

After a long time in custody Paul testifies before several high officials and eventually appeals to have his case heard by Caesar, which is his right as a Roman citizen. Luke is with Paul as they set sail.

Acts 27:1–26

Why don't angels appear every night and tell us what is going on?

Why years in custody and a long boat ride? Why doesn't God make things easier for us to get where we are going?

How does Paul's vision encourage us? How can we encourage those around us?

BIBLE CONVERSATION

Paul shows great courage in the face of danger because he is confident of being part of what the Lord promises long before.

Joel 2:28–32 (Joel 3 in Hebrew text)

Why is the Day of the Lord so important?

Why does Peter use this passage to describe what is happening on the day of Pentecost in Acts 2?

Why is it so important that the Lord pour out his Holy Spirit on us?

Leader Notes

Paul begins his journey to Rome, and it is fraught with the dangers of sailing the Mediterranean in winter. God lets us live our lives and makes us a testimony by the way we respond to the same difficulties as everyone else.

Those who are in Jesus participate in the Lord pouring out his Spirit on all flesh. It is not necessarily like the pouring out at Pentecost. Most others—as the gospel has gone out to the world—have not experienced the same thing. The Lord comes to us according to who we are, where we are, when we live, and what we need.

WEEK 51

Reading 1

BIBLE STORY

Paul, the prisoner on his way to Rome, warns the centurion not to set sail from Crete and now helps them as the ship breaks up. The Lord is with Paul, and he knows it.

Acts 27:27–44

Why is Luke glad that Paul is on the boat?

Why did the soldiers plan to kill the prisoners?

How are real-life adventures different than movies and TV shows?

BIBLE CONVERSATION

Paul continues to speak the message from God during the trial they are going through, because he knows that God is their only salvation.

Hosea 14:4–9 (5–10 in Hebrew text)

What does Paul know from Scripture that will get him through a boat wreck?

What do we know from Scripture that will get us through an impossible day?

What does God want for us?

WEEK 51: READING 1
Leader Notes

Paul has assurance from the Lord that he will bring the gospel to Rome. The gospel is already there, but Paul will one day stand before Caesar.

The Roman soldiers will receive whatever punishment is due to a prisoner if they lose him. They would rather kill them than let them escape. There is no presumption of innocence nor any belief that all humans have equal value. Those in power make the rules to suit themselves, just like now.

The centurion is motivated to get Paul safely to Rome. Centurions are well regarded whenever they appear in the Gospels and Acts.

Hosea expresses God's deep compassion for his people alongside his refusal to accept their sin. The Lord loves us too much to let us act like that.

WEEK 51

Reading 2

BIBLE STORY

After the ship breaks up on Malta, they set sail three months later and reach Rome. Luke's story with Paul ends here, but the gospel has reached all the way to us.

Acts 28

When the snake bites Paul they say he must deserve to die, then that he is a god; what is the truth about Paul?

Why doesn't Paul ever quit telling the good news about Jesus?

BIBLE CONVERSATION

Paul continues to preach the gospel, which is the message of the prophets of old. The Lord has always wanted a changed heart for his people.

Amos 5:21–24

If God commands festivals and sacred assemblies in the Law, why does he hate them?

How would God feel about their religious practices if the people were just and righteous?

Is that the same for us today? How?

WEEK 51: READING 2

Leader Notes

Paul is likely released for a time and then re-arrested, according to 2 Timothy. He may have gone to Spain as he said he wanted to do, but we do not know. Eventually when his case comes before Caesar he loses and is likely imprisoned at the infamous Mamertine Prison in Rome awaiting execution. It is a miserable place and his certainty that his life is at a close is reflected in 2 Timothy. Because Paul is a Roman citizen, he is spared death on a cross and is likely beheaded at dawn outside the city of Rome.

Luke's story is not a biography of Peter or Paul, but rather the story of the gospel starting in Jerusalem and being spread through the main people groups all the way to Rome within a relatively few years.

The festival celebrations of Israel are commanded in the Law of Moses; Israel must observe them. The early church likely continues with Passover, Pentecost, and the Autumn festivals. As with all religious observances, God looks at the heart of the ones celebrating. He never overlooks hypocrisy and sin, but he especially hates it when it is carried out in his name. Paul is a picture of someone who refuses to be part of religious hypocrisy, and like the other apostles, it costs him his earthly life.

WEEK 51

Reading 3

BIBLE STORY

Many years after the Book of Acts ends, the apostle John sees Jesus again on the isle of Patmos. John is now old and falls down to worship the risen, glorified Jesus once again.

Revelation 1

Why does Jesus look so different here than in the Gospels?

Why does John fall at his feet?

Who is this Jesus we follow?

BIBLE CONVERSATION

This Jesus that John sees again is the King foretold by the prophet Micah.

Micah 2:12–13

How is the King also a shepherd?

In what ways are his people like sheep to him?

How does the Lord lead us?

WEEK 51: READING 3

Leader Notes

Jesus appears to John on the island of Patmos where he is in exile. John is quite old. Revelation is the only apocalyptic literature in the New Testament. Ezekiel and Daniel are the main examples of it in the Old Testament.

John, Peter, and James see the glorified Jesus on the mountain in the Gospels. They see the resurrected Jesus more than once. Here at the end of John's life he sees Jesus the King of Heaven.

Micah, long before Jesus, told of this king who leads his people. Jesus is this king who is able to lead his flock past the obstacles that now stop them.

WEEK 52

Reading 1

BIBLE STORY

The glorified Jesus speaks to John on the isle of Patmos regarding seven churches.

Revelation 2

Why does Jesus sound so strict with people who are being persecuted for his sake?

Why do these churches need Jesus' tough honesty?

What might he say about the way we live?

BIBLE CONVERSATION

God wants from his church what he has always wanted—our whole heart.

Micah 6:6–8

Are religious rituals done to impress God or make us pay attention?

What does God really want from us and our rituals?

WEEK 52: READING 1

Leader Notes

Jesus speaks with love and truth. We are used to hearing things designed to entertain us and keep us happy. Truth is hard to hear if we are not used to hearing it. These churches are not geographically far from one another; John knows them.

John will receive a vision of things to come, but the first thing he gets is a message for the churches in the middle of living their lives in a hostile world. Micah long before reinforces that our worship practices done in hypocrisy will not fool God about what is going on in our hearts.

WEEK 52

Reading 2

BIBLE STORY

King Jesus finishes his truthful assessment of the seven churches.

Revelation 3

If Jesus is this direct with his children, how will he be with those who reject him?

Does Jesus love us (Revelation 3:10–13)?

What does he want (Revelation 3:20–22)?

BIBLE CONVERSATION

The last things spoken of in John's revelation concern Israel and the message of the prophets from long ago.

Zechariah 12:9—13:1, 7-9

Who is the son that the inhabitants of Jerusalem will weep over?

What does it mean that the Lord refines and tests his people?

WEEK 52: READING 2

Leader Notes

Jesus continues his incisive assessment of the churches. To the world that rejects him and persecutes his people, he will not even speak. They will be sent away from the Father's house on that great final day.

Zechariah speaks of a terrible day of reckoning and repentance for the nation of Israel when it recognizes, as a nation, Jesus its Messiah.

WEEK 52

Reading 3

BIBLE STORY

After Jesus speaks to John about the churches, John sees a revelation of things to come and the end of all things.

Revelation 21:1–8; 22–27

What will we like about a new heaven and earth?

What will be good about the new Jerusalem?

How do we come to have our names in the Book of Life?

BIBLE CONVERSATION

But before the end, many things will happen.

Malachi 4 (3:19–24 in Hebrew text)

What will it be like to meet Moses and Elijah?

How joyful are newborn calves learning to run (find a video)?

Will you revere the name of the Lord?

WEEK 52: READING 3

Leader Notes

The new heavens and earth are from Isaiah's ancient prophecy. Many of the visions in John's Revelation are from the prophets of Israel. God will bring all things to pass. All accounts will be squared. He will embrace his people and live among them. His people are whomever is written in the Lamb's Book of Life. Jesus is the Lamb of God that takes away the sins of the world. We will live with him forever and ever. Amen.

www.ingramcontent.com/pod-product-compliance
Lightning Source LLC
Chambersburg PA
CBHW071956220426
43662CB00009B/1153